Praise for *The*

T0032141

"Dreamland is the realm of many of our most magical experiences, ranging from psychic epiphanies to communicating with ancestors, loved ones, and angels. Many of my own most profound ancestral experiences, for instance, have occurred in dreams. I'm so grateful to Samantha Fey for *The Awake Dreamer,* which eloquently provides insightful tips and information for enhancing and facilitating the dreaming process, enabling myself and so many others to journey further into ancestor work, as well as our other magical endeavors."

—Judika Illes, author of *Encyclopedia of 5000 Spells, Pure Magic,* and other books

"Samantha's book answers so many questions about the nightlife of us human beings. I *highly* recommend this book to everyone. It unravels the mysteries that we wake up with, trying to understand our dreams, our soul's travels, past-life information and healing. I'm going to recommend this book any chance I get."

—Echo Bodine, author of *How to Live a Happily Ever After Life*

"*The Awake Dreamer* is packed full of fascinating stories, exercises, and techniques to help you recall and work with your dreams. It's well-written, authoritative, helpful, and healing. I thought I was well-read on the subject of dreams but learned a great deal from this remarkable book. It is essential reading for anyone interested in exploring their dreams."

—Richard Webster, author of several books including *Guardian Angels* and *Spirit Guides and Angel Guardians*

"If you've ever felt your dream life was uncharted and even, at times, choppy waters, Samantha Fey is the captain you've been waiting for to help you navigate the mysteries and magic found within it. She expertly and with new insights helps you map out the 'other' life you may have been living without knowing it and empowers you to exclaim: Welcome to the new world!"

—Ryan Singer, writer, comedian, host of *Me and Paranormal You* and creator of the Crystal Eyes App

"Samantha Fey, a gifted intuitive, so wonderfully captures the many aspects of our active dream life in her book, *The Awake Dreamer*. Sharing client experiences and techniques for the reader and supported by research, this practical guide will help you with your own dream interpretation. It will also help you utilize the dream state as an active participant to skillfully journey to find answers, receive guidance, and connect with deceased loved ones as you learn to elevate your dreams.

—Bryn Blankinship, author of *The Limitless Soul*

"In *The Awake Dreamer*, Samantha Fey takes us into some fascinating nooks and crannies of the dreaming mind, while exploring the dreamscape's relationship to out-of-body states, healing, and astral travel. An intrepid guide, Fey's background as a medium gives her a unique vantage to share insights and ponder the imponderable—like do the dead still dream, and if so, are they dreaming of us?

—Lex 'Lonehood' Nover, author of *Nightmareland*

# THE AWAKE DREAMER

# THE AWAKE DREAMER

A Guide to Lucid Dreaming,
Astral Travel, and Mastering
the Dreamscape

SAMANTHA FEY

HAMPTON ROADS

Copyright © 2022
by Samantha Fey

All rights reserved. No part of this publication may be reproduced or
transmitted in any form or by any means, electronic or mechanical, including
photocopying, recording, or by any information storage and retrieval system,
without permission in writing from Red Wheel/Weiser, LLC. Reviewers may
quote brief passages.

Cover design by Kathryn Sky-Peck
Cover image by iStock
Interior by Debby Dutton
Typeset in Adobe Garamond Pro and Incognito

Hampton Roads Publishing Company, Inc.
Charlottesville, VA 22906
Distributed by Red Wheel/Weiser, LLC
www.redwheelweiser.com

Sign up for our newsletter and special offers by going to
www.redwheelweiser.com/newsletter.

ISBN: 978-1-64297-040-1

Library of Congress Cataloging-in-Publication Data available upon request.

Printed in the United States of America
IBI

10 9 8 7 6 5 4 3 2 1

*For my children, Olivia, Victoria, and Chloe–my dreams come true.*

# CONTENTS

# ACKNOWLEDGMENTS

I couldn't have written this book without the encouragement and support of my wonderful agent, Lisa Hagan, and the wonderful team at Hampton Roads. And it would have been impossible to write this book without the enthusiastic help of my daughters. Thank you for never rolling your eyes in the morning when I ask: "Did you have any cool dreams?" And thanks for always being the best, most amazing children any mom could hope for.

To my friend Allison, thank you for being my first reader on so many prior attempts and for your unfailing support on our long walks over the years. Thank you Asia Suler for being a fantastic writer and friend. Your emails, notes, and comments were a tremendous help. A special thank you to my dear friends Tricia, Deb, Denise, Joel, and to my sisters Courtney and Tara for always being there for me.

Finally, I have to acknowledge with infinite gratitude the loyal listeners to my podcasts, *Psychic Teachers* and *Enlightened Empaths*. You all have lifted me up, inspired me, and encouraged my work more than words can express. Thank you for helping me learn to *Be the Light*.

# INTRODUCTION

We all know that dreams can help us solve problems, relieve stress, and inspire creations. But it wasn't until a dream experience I had in the late 1990s that I started to wonder if there was something much more going on when we dream.

One evening, I dreamed I was walking in what appeared to be a subway tunnel with my spirit guide. It was an ordinary tunnel with off-white subway tiles, like Penn Station in New York. In the dream, I walked past a friend who was also walking with her guide. I waved and she returned my greeting. That was the entirety of my dream recall. But for some reason, the vividness of the dream—seeing my friend walking with her guide in this tunnel that felt so familiar to me—stayed with me all day. When I bumped into her at work that afternoon, I told her about it. Before I could finish, she interrupted by finishing my dream story. "I know," she said, "because I had the same dream last night too." How could the two of us have identical dreams on the same night? Had we instead recalled actually having traveled to the other side with our guides?

I've had vivid dreams my whole life. Growing up, I knew I was intuitive. But back then, I chalked up my dreams as part of my active imagination. I dreamed frequently of these glowing beings who visited me at night to bring me comfort. When we moved halfway through my second-grade year, I dreamed that I awoke to find four of these beings seated at the foot of my bed. They were faceless and shapeless, yet they didn't scare me. I never heard them speak aloud; their words simply appeared in my mind. They told me that I would soon have a new teacher. The next day, when I arrived at school, I was told I was being switched from Mrs. Martin's class to Mrs. Burrow's class.

Throughout elementary school, I often dreamed that I visited a special place just for children. I knew that only children were allowed in this safe haven. We met in a building located in a beautiful park nestled in a forest where we could play games or just sit and talk. Some played hopscotch or jumped rope. Others clustered around the pinball machines or basketball hoops, while the younger ones played hide-and-seek. These dreams stopped when I entered middle school, but I never forgot them. Years later, I met one of my best friends at our children's neighborhood play group. As she and I were sitting in a park watching our kids play, for some reason I started telling her about my dreams of a similar place I had dreamed of when I was a child. Just like my co-worker, she started finishing my sentences. "I used to go there too when I was a little girl," she said. We've been friends for almost twenty years now and we still talk about this experience. When we met, I instantly felt as if I knew her and we became fast friends within weeks. Could it be that I had indeed known her from these dream visits when we were children?

Both of these women are intelligent, rational people. My former co-worker has a Ph.D. and describes herself as spiritually agnostic. My play-group friend is a practicing Christian with degrees in science and nursing. I have a master's degree in education and consider myself grounded, smart, and—well, normal. Yet, we three have had these strange, mystical experiences that connect us.

While I was teaching at a community college, I began studying Reiki, a form of hands-on healing. Our Reiki teacher instructed us to meditate each night for twenty-one days to facilitate our healing energy. I'd never meditated with any consistency before this, but, as soon as I started to go within, my dreaming life strengthened dramatically. I dreamed a friend was pregnant a month before she knew. I dreamed my neighbors were moving weeks before the husband got a new job. In a dream, a deceased family member told me an aunt would pass suddenly and unexpectedly.

Then in the summer of 2005, I began having a recurring dream of someone being shot in the neck. I never saw a face in these dreams—just the same horrifying image of a bullet impacting someone's neck. These dreams were always short and always the same. I saw a bullet hitting a man's neck in slow motion, followed by a hand grasping the neck to staunch the flow of blood. At the time, I was married to a police sergeant named Mike who believed he was invincible and rarely wore his bullet-proof vest. After these dreams, I began begging him to wear the vest on his midnight shifts. I also made sure he wore his Archangel Michael medallion for extra protection. When my doorbell rang at 1:00 AM one morning, I think a part of me knew that my dream had come true. Mike had been shot in the neck by a criminal who'd escaped arrest earlier that day.

Many miracles occurred that night that contributed to Mike's survival. As family and friends gathered around me in the hospital to pray with me, I slipped away to the chapel and knelt down. I surrendered all I was and all I feared to God, praying: "Dear God, please let Mike live. If you want me to be an intuitive, I will do that. Help me make sense of these dreams and I will work with you. But please help him live." As a cradle Catholic, making bargains with God came easily to me. Thankfully, God listened, because Mike survived.

Soon after, I signed up for an intuitive development class at a local metaphysical store. Not long after I joined these classes, I began having a series of dreams that I call my "psychic school dreams." I felt as if I were being trained during the day by my teachers and at night by my astral guides. Eventually, I walked away from my secure, wonderful teaching career and embarked on a new path as an intuitive.

As my dream world amplified, it led me to investigate dreams on a much deeper level. But this spiritual awakening was very hard for me. In a short span of time, I went from being a normal wife, mother, and teacher to being this "weird" intuitive working in a small office above a yoga studio. I struggled deeply with my faith and even confessed my new work to a priest. Luckily, he was incredibly kind.

After listening to me "confess" to studying tarot, crystals, and mediumship, he paused for a moment and said: "So what are your sins, my dear?"

I stumbled over my response before blurting out: "Didn't I just confess them?"

The elderly priest smiled at me and leaned forward on his elbows. "Tell me this," he said. "Do you keep God at the center of all you do?" When I acknowledged that I did, he said: "Then go in peace."

As I left the church, I thought: "Samantha, you've been given permission to do this work, both in your dreams and now by this holy person. So go forth in peace as he told you to."

And that's what I did. And in my work, I kept coming across people who were just like me. Clients poured in who were fascinated by this esoteric world, but were afraid to pursue it due to their religious beliefs. This left us all feeling lost, alone, and disconnected. When I talked about this conundrum with a friend who was a practicing Pagan, a university teacher, and my tarot mentor, she admitted to remaining "in the closet" with her work, fearing the university would fire her. When I confronted her with my belief that there were a lot of people like us—normal, smart, educated people of faith who still wanted to learn about the mysteries of life—she replied: "Let me know when you find them."

And that's how we started our podcast, *Psychic Teachers,* an endeavor that has grown over the years into a supportive community of intuitives learning together how to navigate this spiritual journey called life. I began sharing my dream experiences on the show each week and emails began flooding in with listeners' own dream stories of astral travel, lucid dreaming, meeting loved ones on the other side, and encountering angelic beings.

## SOUL TRAVEL

As my dreaming world expanded and I began to offer healings, readings, and to help earth bound spirits cross over, I started calling myself a "nightworker." I felt as if I were a "lightworker" in my day job, helping to shed light on people's problems, grief, and questions. But at night, I knew my soul was journeying beyond this earthly realm to continue this work. Yet my studies into the world of dreams led me to realize that the term "nightworker" wasn't inclusive enough to describe what was actually occurring. Now I call these dream experiences "soul traveling," because this is what happens to us when our bodies rest. Each night as we sleep, our souls leave our bodies and travel. Some may visit family members, or friends, or co-workers. Others journey even farther and engage with their guides, with angels, or with loved ones on the other side.

I believe we are all soul travelers. There's a wonderful old legend about souls in heaven waiting to be born. God greets each of them to say goodbye and prepare them for life on Earth. But the souls are already feeling homesick and complain that they will miss heaven and God's presence. God comforts them, saying: "Don't be sad. Each night when you fall asleep, your soul returns here. Go with my blessing and know that you will visit me each night when sleep delivers you home." Personal experience and research have taught me that there's a lot of truth to this ancient tale.

Freud called dreams "the royal road to knowledge of the unconscious activities of the mind." Jung believed dreams were "impartial, spontaneous products of the unconscious psyche." Yet even Jung had a dream six weeks after his father's death that made him rethink the possibility of an afterlife. And while I agree that most of these dreams are merely outlets for our subconscious, my experience has taught me that, many nights, we travel in our dreams to places beyond this earthly realm. During these soul travels, we remain connected to our bodies by a silver cord of energy. Most of these "dreams" are visits to the other side where we can rest or review our soul's plan. And some people spend this time helping others by offering healing, advice, and support.

Soul travelers have dreams that are very different from average dreamers. They tend to be incredibly vivid, colorful, and chronological. They feel more like visits and have a clear beginning, a middle, and an end. Soul travelers often wake up feeling more tired than when they went to sleep. Individuals who are focused on helping others—either through healing work, creative endeavors, or intuitive guidance—tend to be natural soul travelers.

In the chapters that follow, I share with you the experiences and stories of many who, throughout the ages, have soul traveled to the other side and brought back insight, messages, and healing to help us harness the power of our dreams. I also include stories shared with me by my friends and clients, experiences of my own, and some simple exercises that can help you activate the soul traveler in you.

# Chapter 1

# FAMOUS SOUL TRAVELERS

*The dream is a little hidden door in the innermost and most secret recesses of the soul, opening into that cosmic night.*

Carl Jung

Have you ever had a dream that later came true? Or perhaps you dreamed of your grandmother visiting you from heaven. Have you ever dreamed of a past life that felt more real than your own memories? Or had a shared dream experience with a close friend?

Every major religion and culture teaches that we are all made up of three components—our bodies, our minds, and our souls. But what happens to us while our bodies sleep? Where do our souls go? Could it be that when our bodies and minds are resting, our souls travel to visit with friends, meet with guides and loved ones on the other side, or explore different astral dimensions?

# ANCIENT AND MODERN
# DREAMERS

Throughout history, dreams have been researched, recorded, and examined for the treasure of information they hold. The first recorded dream dates back to 2700 BCE, when the Sumerian King Gudea dreamed he saw men and women carrying large objects with the help of animals. He interpreted this as a sign that the gods wanted him to build a temple. In ancient Egypt, priests known as "masters of secret things" interpreted the dreams of the faithful. The Chester Beatty papyrus includes a record of Egyptian dream interpretations dating back to 1800 BCE. In India, the *Athavaveda* (fifth century BCE) contains a chapter on dreams and omens. Dream diviners called "examiners of dreams" worked in ancient China, while the ancient Greeks and Romans brought dream interpreters to war with them, believing that dreams were messages from the gods that could help them win battles.

The Talmud contains over 200 references to dreams and there are more than twenty dreams referenced in the Bible. Jacob dreams of seeing angels descending from heaven via a ladder. Later, he's warned in a dream to return home. God appears to King Solomon in a dream, offering him anything he wants. Solomon chooses wisdom. An angel appears to Joseph in a dream to soothe his fears about Mary's virgin conception. The three Magi are warned in a dream not to return to Harrod. Before the crucifixion, Pilate's wife has a dream telling her that Jesus is innocent. In the East, Buddha's mother dreams that an elephant entered her womb and told her her son would be a universal monarch.

Belief in the supernatural power of dreams is found across many cultures and religions. In ancient Greece, people practiced "temple sleep," or dream incubation, in which the sick visited oracular temples to perform rites intended to help them receive insight and healing in dreams. The hope was that they would encounter a god or guide in these dreams who would offer healing advice. In *The Dreamer's Book of the Dead*, Robert Moss tells us: "Greeks used the term *oneiros* not only for 'dream' but as the term for a living entity or energy that travels to dreamers during the night."

In the world of dreams, inventors have discovered new techniques, scientists have conjured new medicines to heal the sick, and artists have created poetry, plays, and music. Harriet Tubman was guided by dreams to make her escape from slavery and continued to be guided by her dreams to return south and lead others to freedom via the Underground Railroad. Elias Howe invented the sewing machine thanks to insight received in a dream. Lucille Ball dreamed that her deceased friend, the famous actress Carol Lombard, told her to take a chance on the *I Love Lucy* show. Frederick Banting's dream led to the invention of insulin.

Novels like *Frankenstein*, *Misery*, *Dr. Jekyll and Mr. Hyde*, *Twilight*, and the *Harry Potter* books are all rooted in powerful dreams gifted to the authors. After E. B. White finished his novel *Stuart Little*, he wrote to his agent:

I will have to break down and confess to you that Stuart Little appeared to me in a dream—all complete with his hat, his cane and his brisk manner. Since he was the only fictional character ever to honor and disturb my sleep, I was deeply touched and felt I was not free to change him into a grasshopper or wallaby.

Music has also been created in dreams. Paul McCartney famously dreamed the melody to "Yesterday." Keith Richards wrote the lyrics to "Satisfaction" in a dream. Billy Joel admitted that all the music he ever composed came from dreams.

Many have reported being visited by loved ones in dreams and encouraged to bring messages of healing or warnings to prevent upcoming disasters. Mark Twain dreamed of his brother's tragic death weeks before it happened. Stories of precognitive dreams—some filled with wonder and hope, and others foretelling impending misfortunes—have been recorded for centuries.

Even though history is full of evidence of soul travelers, dream research didn't really become serious until the 1950s. As Chip Brown writes in the *Smithsonian Magazine:* "It remains an astonishing anachronism in the history of science that Watson and Crick unraveled the structure of DNA before virtually anything was known about the physiological condition in which people spend one-third of their lives."

In 1953, sleep researchers Eugene Aserinsky and Nathaniel Kleitman revealed that we dream during the

REM (rapid eye movement) sleep cycle. When researchers woke people during their REM cycles, participants recalled their dreams easily compared with participants who were awakened during non-REM sleep periods. Research has shown that, on average, 80 percent of people recall dreams if they are woken during the REM cycle, which usually starts one to two hours after they fall asleep. Before Aserinsky and Kleitman's groundbreaking paper, scientists saw sleeping as a passive state unworthy of research. After their work, scientists began studying dreams as what they called a "third state of being."

## SWEDENBORG

One of the most famous soul travelers is Emanuel Swedenborg, who is often referred to as the "Scandinavian DaVinci." Born in 1688 to a wealthy Swedish family, he was so brilliant that he began taking university classes when he was just eleven years old. As a child, he often spoke of unseen playmates he called "the boys in the garden." His parents were shocked by the wise, spiritual stories he shared and believed he was talking to angels. While still a child, he learned how to do a special kind of breathwork that slowed his breathing so much that it appeared as if he weren't breathing at all. This breath technique most likely prepared him for soul traveling in the dream state.

After graduating from college, where he mastered nine languages and acquired extensive expertise in math and science, Swendenborg traveled to England to continue his scientific studies. He set up an alchemical lab on London

Bridge and founded an esoteric school after studying with Rabbi Falk, who many researchers believe sowed the seeds for the future Golden Dawn society. During this time, he traveled throughout Europe and stayed in several Jewish communities, where he studied the Kabbalah. But he kept these esoteric studies hidden. On the outside, he was known as a scientist and engineer. In secret, he was studying the Kabbalah and alchemy, and practicing breathwork.

In his fifties, Swedenborg underwent a profound spiritual awakening in which he experienced moments of ecstasy, fainting spells, and dreams of heaven and hell. While trying to fall asleep, he heard a noise in his head that sounded like a gush of wind. This triggered a soul-traveling dream in which he met with Jesus Christ, who told him to abandon his pursuit of science and focus on his esoteric work. He describes the experience in his book *Heaven and Hell*:

> That same night were opened to me so that
> I became thoroughly convinced of their real-
> ity—the world of spirits—heaven and hell. And
> I recognized their many acquaintances of every
> condition in life. From that day, I gave up the
> study of all worldly science and labored on spiri-
> tual things according as the Lord commanded me
> to write. Afterward, the Lord opened daily, very
> often, my bodily eyes so that, in the middle of
> the day, I could see into the other world and, in a
> state of perfect wakefulness, converse with angels
> and spirits.

Swedenborg's dreams taught him that God was love and that he wanted all of us to share in this love. He said God is never angry and would never judge us or send us to hell. He explained that people go to hell because that's where they want to be and said that heaven and hell looked very much like our world, with gardens, houses, rivers, streams, and flowers. People in heaven, he said, eat, laugh, and make love. But hell is a squalid, dark, and depressing place filled with negative, angry people. He explained that, in these realms, we create our reality with our thoughts through a kind of instant manifestation.

Swendenborg's soul travels revealed a metaphysical concept that wouldn't be taught until the 20th century. Rejecting the fire-and-brimstone teachings of religion, he claimed that his soul travels revealed that, upon death, we go to the level of heaven that resonates with the person we were in life. Instead of facing eternal judgment, we are drawn like a magnet to the level of the afterlife that resonates with our true essence. We can call these levels heaven, purgatory, or hell, but in reality, there are countless levels. Murderers are drawn to an empty, nasty, depressing landscape because that's what resonates with their true souls. Power hungry souls are drawn to a competitive afterlife, while those who spent their lives on earth sharing kindness and instinctively giving from a place of altruism are drawn to the higher realms. Through his soul travels, Swedenborg learned that time doesn't exist on the other side. It's measured—not in hours, days, or weeks—but in each individual's state of mind. We travel in the spirit world by thinking about where we want to go.

Swendenborg's soul travels taught him that, when people first enter the spiritual world, they meet friends or relatives who crossed over before them. In *Heaven and Hell*, he writes:

> Spouses will be reunited, although not necessarily forever. The spiritual world is a place where a person's inner nature becomes the whole of their being. If two people were truly of one mind on earth, they will live together as spouses in heaven too. However, if they were not happily married, or if their personalities are fundamentally different, they will eventually part ways.

Those who did not find love on earth, he says, will eventually find their perfect match in heaven—no one is ever alone unless they wish to be. Friends and relatives become the new arrivals' guides to the spiritual world.

In his book *The Lives of Angels*, Swedenborg writes of his visits to the other side, where he says that everything is constructed from thought and God's light. He describes how spirits and angels in heaven work in groups—some to help newly crossed souls acclimate to the other side, some to help souls understand divine wisdom, and some to help protect us on Earth. Some brave souls even work in the hellish realms to bring enlightenment to souls there.

Swedenborg's dreams carried over into his waking life, which is often the case for soul travelers. His dreams and visions awakened a latent psychic ability within him. When he met the Queen of Sweden, she asked him if he had ever encountered her deceased brother on the other side. He said he had not, but that he would try. He returned to court a few days later to relay a message from her brother. He whispered something in the Queen's ear to which she replied: "No one but God knows this secret."

Like other soul travelers, Swedenborg accessed his true spiritual nature through the dream state, uniting his body, mind, and spirit, and awakening his psychic abilities. Edgar Cayce, who became known as the Sleeping Prophet, did this as well.

## EDGAR CAYCE

Edgar Cayce was born in Kentucky in 1877, one of six children. Like Swedenborg, he claimed to play with invisible friends as a child. Cayce was known for his devout faith and kindness, but he struggled with his schoolwork. One evening when his father was drilling him on his spelling words, Cayce heard a voice telling him to "sleep a little" so he could access the help and information he needed to pass his exams. He fell asleep with his spelling book tucked under his pillow. When he awoke, he could remember everything in the book. He learned to pass all his courses by sleeping on his textbooks, giving new meaning to the adage: "Sleep on it." By the end of the year, Cayce had become a star student.

Soon after this experience, he came down with a severe case of laryngitis that the doctors couldn't cure. One evening while under hypnosis, he began to diagnose his own illness. His vocal cords, he said, were partially paralyzed but, with circulation directed to that area, he'd be cured. The diagnosis proved accurate and Cayce made a full recovery. And so the Sleeping Prophet was born.

Each day, Cayce entered a trance-like sleep state and gave readings while his wife guided him and a stenographer recorded his messages. In his lifetime, he gave over 14,000 readings that are housed today at the Association for Research and Enlightenment in Virginia. These readings contain information about health and diet, records of past lives, predictions of future lives, premonitions, and even information about the ancient history of our planet. Cayce reported, for example, that the Akashic Records, which contain all this knowledge, are stored in a secret chamber under the Sphinx in Egypt. He also is said to have predicted the Great Depression and World War II.

Today, people still study the information Cayce shared from his soul travels to learn about our life purpose, to facilitate medical breakthroughs, and to gain insight into the future of our planet. Cayce remained a devout Christian throughout his life and never took credit for the messages that came through while he was in his trance-like state. Even though presidents, foreign heads of state, and other influential people sought him out, he remained humble and unassuming, and never earned more than eighty-five dollars a week.

But if Cayce could travel to distant worlds during the sleep state to gain healing advice and receive accurate premonitions, doesn't it stand to reason tha we can also use the dream world to connect with loved ones who've transitioned to the other side? The simple answer is yes. We'll discuss this aspect of soul travel in chapter 3. For now, let's look at the fascinating inner life of another soul traveler to see how soul traveling can help us connect with our spirit guides and angels.

## WILLIAM BLAKE

William Blake was born into a working-class family in London in 1757. He left school when he was ten, but later studied at the Royal Academy for six years. He supported himself as a professional engraver, but is best remembered as a poet and painter. Blake himself believed that many of his artistic creations were inspired by his dreams of a man with a third eye who showed him what to paint. He even drew an image of this man with the innocuous title: "Man Who Instructed Blake in Painting His Dreams."

As a struggling artist, Blake needed to find a way to sell more of his work. One night, when he fell asleep thinking about this problem, his deceased brother Robert came to him in a dream and showed him a way to etch images onto metal plates using chemicals so he could sell more copies of them. The new technique, which he called "illuminated printing," worked and allowed Blake to continue his career successfully. When a friend of his lost a son, Blake consoled him in a letter by sharing his own experiences after his brother's death.

I know that our deceased friends are more really with us than when they were apparent to our mortal part. Thirteen years ago I lost a brother, and with his spirit I converse daily and hourly in the spirit, and see him in my remembrance, in the region of my imagination. I hear his advice, and even now write from his dictate.

In *The Life of William Blake*, Alexander Gilchrist quotes a letter from Blake to Thomas Butts that tells of the poet seeing visions in dreams, meeting with deceased friends while in the dream state, and having prophetic dream encounters.

Now I may say to you, what perhaps I should not dare to say to anyone else: That I can alone carry on my visionary studies in London unannoyed, and that I may converse with my friends in eternity, see visions, dreams and prophecy and speak parables unobserved and at liberty from the doubts of other mortals; perhaps doubts proceeding from kindness, but doubts are always pernicious, especially when we doubt our friends.

Blake rarely struggled with his own doubts. He understood that his visions and dreams were real, perhaps more real than the life he experienced in London. "The world of imagination," he wrote, "is the world of eternity."

Like many well-known soul travelers, Blake grew up seeing visions of angels and helpers. He often spoke of seeing angels helping people with their daily lives and dreamed of meeting Mother Mary, the archangels, and saints in his dreams—all of whom inspired his writing and art. Like other famous soul travelers, he used his dream life to channel inspiring work and to influence new teachings about the way consciousness works. One of these fellow travelers was Carl Jung.

## CARL JUNG

Carl Jung is considered the most influential psychologist of our times. He explored the world of dreams, art, religion, and mythology to explain what he called "the collective unconscious." His autobiography, *Memories, Dreams, and Reflections*, gives us fascinating insights into his soul travels.

In 1926, Jung dreamed that he was an alchemist in the 17th century. This led him to see alchemy, not as the transmutation of lead into gold, but as the transformation of the soul into our higher selves. In *Memories, Dreams, and Reflections*, he writes about experiencing dream visions while recovering from a heart attack:

> It was as if I were in an ecstasy. I felt as though I were floating in space, as though I were safe in the womb of the universe in a tremendous void but filled with the highest possible feeling of happiness. Everything around me seemed enchanted. Night after night I floated in a state of purest bliss, thronged round with images of all creation.

He dreamed of what he called a "mystical marriage" that allowed him to explore the yin/yang union more fully. He also dreamed of meeting a Hindu and encountering a dwarf in a cave, where he found a red crystal. He often dreamed of and conversed with a man named Philemon, who Jung believed was a type of spirit guide for him.

After his father died, Jung encountered him in several dreams that felt so real that they led him to rethink his beliefs about life after death. He wrote:

> Six weeks after his death, my father appeared to me in a dream. Suddenly he stood before me and said that he was coming back from his holiday. He had made a good recovery and was now coming home. I thought he would be annoyed with me for having moved into his room. But not a bit of it! Nevertheless, I felt ashamed because I had imagined he was dead. Two days later the dream was repeated. My father had recovered and was coming home, and again I reproached myself because I had thought he was dead. Later I kept asking myself: "What does it mean that my father returns in dreams and that he seems so real?" It was an unforgettable experience, and it forced me for the first time to think about life after death. (*Memories, Dreams, and Reflections*)

In 1913, Jung began dreaming about terrifying visions of a devastated Europe. He wrote;

> I saw a monstrous flood covering all the north-ern and low-lying lands between the North Sea and the Alps. When it came up to Switzerland, I saw that the mountains grew higher and higher

to protect our country. I realized that a frightful catastrophe was in progress. I saw mighty yellow waves, the floating rubble of civilization, and the drowned bodies of uncounted thousands. Then the whole sea turned to blood. Two weeks passed; then the vision recurred, under the same conditions, even more vividly than before, and the blood was more emphasized. An inner voice spoke. "Look at it well; it is wholly real and it will be so. You cannot doubt it." (*Memories, Dreams, and Reflections*)

Later that spring, he had three more dreams in which he saw all of Europe covered in ice.

Jung believed these dreams predicted the beginnings of World War I. The "mighty yellow waves" he saw as images of the mustard gas used in that war. The rising mountains protecting his country most likely symbolized Switzerland's neutrality during the war, and surely the sea of blood predicted the deaths of over nine million soldiers during those awful years. Possibly the "frozen wasteland" predicted the war's wintry end in November 1918.

In 1922, Jung had a dream in which his father came to him asking about the psychology of marriage. He assigned no particular meaning to it until two months later, when he had a terrifying dream of a wolf carrying away a soul. He awoke in the morning to the news that his mother had died. Jung believed his father had come to him in a dream asking about marriage to warn him of his mother's impending demise.

Jung's dreams and visions helped form the foundation for his views on the key components of his philosophy—the collective unconscious, archetypes, the shadow self, and the depths of the subconscious mind. Swedenborg's dreams taught him about the reality of life after death. Blake's brought with them a new and deeper understanding of the angelic realm and enriched his poetry and painting. Cayce's established psychic ability as a real, invaluable resource for help and enlightenment.

Just think what soul traveling could do for you.

**Exercise: Your Dream Team**
Napoleon Hill, author of bestselling books like *Think and Grow Rich,* developed the technique of consulting what he called his "invisible council." He chose nine deceased people whom he greatly admired. As he fell asleep, he imagined talking with these souls to seek their advice and input. He called this visualization technique his "nightly meetings" and never wrote a word or prepared a speech without first consulting this group.

In fact, this technique proved so successful that Hill became afraid he was indulging his imagination too much, so he put a stop to his nightly meetings. Soon after, he dreamed that President Lincoln, a member of his council, visited him and told him to recommence the meetings, because they had important work to do together. He did just that and went on to pen over a dozen bestselling books that are still in print today.

You can create your own "dream team" of wise people you admire and conduct dream meetings with your own personal council as you drift off to sleep. Choose nine people from history who exemplify characteristics you deem helpful. For example, you could ask William Blake to provide creative inspiration, or you could ask Joan of Arc to council you on resiliency and courage. Perhaps Martin Luther King, Jr. could fill you with faith, unity, and justice. Dorothy Parker could add humor and spice to your meetings, while Eleanor Roosevelt could give you the wisdom and perseverance needed to see your goals through to fruition. Frederick Douglass could add intelligence, commitment, and inspiration.

After you've chosen your team, write down their names in your dream journal. Do some research on each individual. As you fall asleep each night, visualize yourself sitting in a beautiful conference room, a cozy living room, or an ornate library. Invite each member to join you. Make this visualization as real as possible. Engage each of your senses as you imagine greeting each member. Discuss a problem or situation that is weighing on your mind. See yourself sipping tea or coffee with your council as you listen for their guidance. Give them permission to continue counseling you in your dreams.

When you wake in the morning, take a moment to sit and process any dreams you had. Write down any thoughts, impressions, feelings, or memories you can call to mind from your dream time. As you consult with your dream team on a consistent basis, you'll start to receive more accurate and vivid guidance, until eventually these "imaginary" nightly meetings are as real as (but a lot more fun than) a typical workday meeting.

# Chapter 2

# PREMONITORY DREAMS

*In the Universe there are things that are known,*
*and things that are unknown, and in between,*
*there are doors.*

William Blake

When Judy was ten, she dreamed that a classmate who had moved away returned and showed up in her classroom. The next day, this scenario played out in real life. The girl walked right up to her and said: "Hi! I've moved back" just like in her dream. EMS officer Paul dreamed that a call came over the radio describing a man who had died in a motorcycle accident. The next night, that exact same call came through and Paul was first to arrive on the scene. Juanita had a dream in which she was driving to work when four lions appeared on the highway blocking the road. The next day, she decided to take a different route to work and later discovered there was a four-car accident on the road she would have taken if she hadn't heeded her dream.

What do all these dreams mean? Can we harness their power to prevent or prepare for tragedies or other events in our own lives? And how can we tell the difference between a dream and a premonition?

## PREMONITIONS

We've all experienced dreams about showing up late for an exam, or being naked in public, or flying, or tumbling down stairs. And these dreams can give us insight into our anxieties, worries, and fears. They allow our innermost selves the freedom to express themselves.

But premonitory dreams are different. They usually center around people or places who are familiar to us; they have a sense of reality to them. Upon waking, many report knowing that a dream was a premonition and not the result of suppressed fears. The scenarios play out in chronological order—something that doesn't often happen in traditional dreams. Studies show that about 30 percent of us have had premonitory dreams that later came true.

Premonitions often act as vehicles for information when traditional modes of communication aren't working. When a client's uncle was caught in a huge storm in Hawaii, all the phone lines went down. His family was worried about him and prayed he had made it through the storm. That night, my client had a dream that her uncle called. "Can you hear me?" he asked. "It's your uncle. I can't talk long. I just wanted you to know I am safe. Tell the family." The next day, her uncle called to report that he was okay, just as had happened in her dream.

A mother's intuition is a powerful thing. When Linda's daughter was studying overseas, she sometimes went days without hearing from her. One night, she dreamed that her daughter had fallen down a cliffside and broken her ankle but was okay. The next day, her daughter called to tell her exactly that.

Mothers often report having premonitions like Linda's. Natasha had a dream that her son had been in a mountain-bike accident. Because of her dream, she was able to find him and get him to the hospital in time. Some mothers have premonitions before the birth of a child. When Rebecca was pregnant, she dreamed that her baby would be born early. Because of this, she was prepared when she went into labor three weeks before her due date.

Premonitions are often a sign that you have strong intuitive abilities. When Kenya was thirteen, she had a very specific premonitory dream about a man walking up and down the aisles of a liquor store. She watched him as he walked up to the register, pulled out a gun, and robbed the store. The next day when she watched the evening news, she saw that the exact store in her dream had been robbed that night. She is now a practicing intuitive who works with law enforcement on cold cases.

Sometimes premonitions occur to warn us or prepare us for future events. Jennifer has premonitory dreams before family members die. She had a dream in which her aunt was explaining to her that she was ready to move on. Her aunt died unexpectedly the following week.

Does this mean that the future is set in stone? Millions of people visit psychics, astrologers, and palmists hoping for a glimpse into their future. After doing readings for almost two decades, I have learned that predicting the future is tricky because it's malleable and susceptible to the choices we make (or choose not to make). Imagine that life is like an elaborate system of highways, routes, and lanes. If you are driving along a highway when an accident occurs up the road a bit, you will come across this accident *if* you stay on the highway. But you also have the choice of getting off at an exit and taking a different route. It is our choices that ultimately determine our future. A skilled, ethical intuitive will never predict your future. Instead, they will show you your options—the highways and byways that await you in the future.

My recurring dream about someone being shot in the neck is a good case in point. It gave me a tantalizing glimpse of the future, but didn't provide me with any specifics. I later learned that an ambulance showed up at the scene of the shooting right away because it had been summoned to the neighborhood by a prank call. The doctors told me that this prank call saved Mike's life. Moreover, the thoracic surgeon he needed was waiting at the hospital, having just finished up another emergency procedure, and the precise type of blood Mike needed for his transfusions was right there where they needed it. So many things lined up for Mike to survive that night. It's made me wonder if some aspects of our lives are, in fact, pre-destined.

The debate over destiny versus free will has been ongoing throughout the ages. I've often felt sorry for Calvinists who believe that everything is set in stone—even the fate of your soul—before you take one breath of life. Through the years of doing readings, I have learned that the Calvinists are wrong . . . and right. Some parts of our life plan are destined, while the majority of our life events are determined by our free will. In fact, I've come to believe that premonitory dreams may be aspects of our souls that remember pre-destined events that we planned before coming to Earth.

## THE COLLECTIVE UNCONSCIOUS

I've always pictured Jung's collective unconscious as an elaborate web of energy woven within, through, and around our planet. "The collective unconscious, which sends you these dreams," Jung said in an interview, "already possesses the solution: nothing has been lost from the whole immemorial experience of humanity, every imaginable situation and every solution seem to have been foreseen by the collective unconscious." When we're tuned into this collective unconscious through awareness of the present moment, heightened intuition, and clarity of mind through meditation, we can access information channeled through this grid of energy that surrounds all of us.

When we examine premonitory dreams, it becomes apparent that the majority predict fearful events— impending illnesses, death, catastrophes, or accidents. But why do so many premonitions foretell negative events? The Global Consciousness Project, which began at Princeton University in 1988, may provide some answers. The project was designed to see if global consciousness had an effect on physical systems. Using a system of random-number generators, researchers led by experimental psychologist Roger D. Nelson wanted to determine if global events registered on the system, thereby proving that our collective energy does indeed impact us all.

The researchers posted a network of seventy random-number generators, nicknamed "Princeton Eggs," around the world. Every second, the generators electronically choose a new random number and the results are recorded. The group then analyzes the data looking for anomalies. When numbers are skewed from their normal pattern, the researchers look to see if a world event could have triggered this, suggesting that the collective electromagnetic energy of our thoughts and emotions impact the world around us.

The study showed a huge spike in the numbers starting around four hours before the attacks on 9-11, and again at the exact moment the first tower was hit. Likewise, the numbers went off the charts just before the Indian Ocean tsunami and spiked immediately before the American embassy was attacked in Africa. Anomalies were also recorded when Princess Diana died and again on the day of her funeral. Researchers have determined that the statistical probability of these being chance occurrences is one in a trillion, thus showing that, yes, Virginia, there is a collective consciousness into which we can all tap.

## GLIMPSES OF THE FUTURE

Perhaps the reason why many premonitions are negative in nature is simply because we are all tapping into the collective consciousness, which is usually rooted in fear. If we are biologically wired to be on the alert for fight or flight stressors to ensure the survival of the species, then it makes sense that the majority of premonitions would be filled with ominous warnings.

Many people had fearful premonitions before 9-11. In fact, the four planes that crashed on that day were only about 20 percent full. Numerous studies have reported that a significant number of people had dreams of "planes crashing into buildings," or "planes disappearing into a silver mountain," or "looking out from a high building as a plane approached too closely."

One of the first people to research premonitory dreams seriously was English psychiatrist John Barker. Following the Aberfan landslide in 1966, which killed nearly 150 children and adults when waste from a coal mine buried a school in South Wales, Barker started the Premonitions Bureau to record people's glimpses into the future, hoping to learn more about the powerful information we could glean from these future-telling dreams. When he spoke to town residents, he realized that many of them had experienced some type of premonition about the disaster. Even some of the children who died in the tragedy mentioned having premonitions of dying in the days before the landslide. Eryl Mai woke up one day before the disaster to tell her mom about a disturbing dream she had in which she arrived at school to find the building gone. She said: "Something black had come down all over it."

When Barker solicited reports of premonitions about the disaster, he received sixty responses. One woman recorded this dream:

> An old schoolhouse nestling in a valley, then a Welsh miner, then an avalanche of coal hurtling down a mountainside. At the bottom of this mountain of hurtling coal was a little boy with a long fringe looking absolutely terrified to death. Then for a while I "saw" rescue operations taking place. I had an impression that the little boy was left behind and saved. He looked so grief-stricken. I could never forget him, and also with him was one of the rescue workers wearing an unusual, peaked cap.

When she later watched a television news report, the woman was shocked to see both the terrified boy from her dream and his rescuer in the news footage. Since then, people have accurately reported dreams of airline crashes, horse races, and even RFK's assassination to the Premonition Bureau. But the spookiest thing to come out of the Barker's work is that two respondents correctly predicted his own untimely death at the age of forty-four.

## HARBINGERS OF DEATH

Many people have experienced premonitory dreams about death. Mark Twain may have been right when he said there are only two things we can count on—death and taxes.

Indeed, his famous quote may have been the result of his own dreams. When he was younger, Twain and his brother, Henry, worked on steamboats traveling the Mississippi River from New Orleans to Ohio. One night when he was staying with his sister, Twain dreamed he was at his brother's funeral. He saw his brother laid out in a metal coffin resting across two chairs. Henry was wearing his brother's suit. Twain noticed a bouquet of white flowers with a single red rose in the center lying across his chest. When Twain awoke, he was so disturbed that he went for a walk to shake off the frightening reality of the dream and clear it from his energy. He told his sister, his friends—anyone who'd listen—about the dream, but everyone assured him that Henry was alive and well.

Sadly, Henry died soon after when a boiler exploded on the riverboat *Pennsylvania*. When Twain arrived at his brother's funeral, he was shocked to find him laid out in his borrowed suit, resting in a metal coffin positioned across two chairs. The only thing missing was the bouquet of white flowers with the single red rose at the center. As Twain stood by his brother's coffin, a woman approached to pay her respects. She laid a bouquet of white flowers on Henry's chest—with a single red rose in the center.

Some report having premonitions about their own demise. When the father of a friend of mine was in the hospital recovering from a heart attack, she went to visit him one afternoon and told him he would be coming home soon. Her dad shook his head and said: "No, I'm going to my true home tonight. An angel visited me in my dreams last night and said she was coming to take me home." My friend shook her head, refusing to believe him. She left to find his doctor, who assured her that her father was doing fine and would most likely be released by the end of the week. A nurse who overheard their exchange said: "That's odd. Two other patients told me they had the same dream last night." The doctor replied that the strange dreams were most likely caused by medication. But my friend's father and those two other patients died that night.

It may be that our birth and death dates are indeed a part of our destiny. Throughout my marriage, I was very close to my mother-in-law. When she died in 2007, I was devastated, having lost both a mother figure and a dear friend. But soon she began appearing to me in dreams. One dream in particular has always made me question everything I thought I knew to be true about life and death.

I dreamed that I woke up and walked into my kitchen. My mother-in-law was standing there with one of her closest friends and I remember feeling as if I knew exactly why they were there. They were animated and excited. Then the friend looked at me and said: "I've decided it's time for me to join Maggie in heaven." When I woke up, I couldn't shake the dream and shared it with my husband, telling him that I thought his mother's friend was going to die soon. He was skeptical, saying that the friend was perfectly healthy and had no health issues. But six weeks later she died in her sleep from a brain aneurism.

This experience left me feeling a little guilty. Was there something I should or could have done to prevent this death? And, in fact, this is one of the negative aspects of premonitory dreams. Many recipients of negative dream premonitions are left feeling as if they should have done something to prevent the disaster, death, or upheaval predicted in their dreams. But in all of these scenarios, there is nothing that can be done.

A client emailed to tell me that she'd had dream premonitions before the death of every one of her relatives, leaving her with the family nickname "the Grim Reaper." She said she feels almost responsible for these deaths, even though she understands on a rational level that this is impossible. If our higher selves, our souls, understand why we're here and when we're supposed to leave Earth, then it makes sense that, during the dream state, when our souls are free to travel, we can journey to our intuitive friends—people who are tapped into the collective consciousness—to say our goodbyes.

Still, these experiences can leave us feeling weighted down with a sense of responsibility and even guilt. The night before a big fight, heavy-weight boxer Sugar Ray Robinson dreamed that he would land a series of punches to his opponent, Jimmy Doyle, and be declared the winner. But in the dream, to his horror, he saw that Doyle was dead. When he awoke the next morning, Robinson called his promoter and begged him to call off the fight. When he refused, Robinson called the boxing commission. They refused as well and instead sent a priest to allay Robinson's fears. The fight occurred as planned and Robinson knocked out Doyle in the eighth round. Doyle was carried out on a stretcher and died the next day. Many friends say Robinson never got over this experience.

The guilt that premonitory dreams can leave behind can be very hard to shake off. I believe strongly that some things are destined to be and are not for us to question or even understand. All we can do is pray and ask for guidance, discernment, and inner wisdom when making the choices that are ours to make through our free will.

Prayer has been shown to have a powerful effect on our dreams and our ability to soul travel. When Major Archibald Gracie stood on the deck of the Titanic as it was sinking, he knew he wouldn't find a spot on a lifeboat. As he sank into the icy water, he began to pray that his spirit would somehow visit his wife and family to say goodbye before he succumbed. At that exact moment, his wife was drifting off to sleep in their home. She heard a voice say: "On your knees and pray." She later said: "Instantly, I literally obeyed with my prayer book in hand which, by chance, opened at the prayer *For Those at Sea*. The thought then flashed through my mind, 'Archie is praying for me.'" Major Gracie miraculously found an overturned lifeboat and survived.

## GLAD TIDINGS

Although the majority of premonitory dreams forecast death or doom, some are filled with happy predictions of wonderful events coming our way. When my sister announced her engagement to her boyfriend, my parents were delighted at first—until she announced that she'd be converting from Catholicism to the Greek Orthodoxy. Then they were furious and refused to pay for the wedding or even attend. So my sister planned the wedding on her own; she and her fiancé saved all year to pay for it. Then one night, shortly before the big day, she dreamed that three elderly women walked into her home filled with good cheer and celebration. The oldest of the three, who was clearly in charge, told her all would be well. "Just you wait and see," she said. "Soon your dad will call with good news." The next day, her dad called to say that they would attend the ceremony after all. And their wedding gift? A check to cover the cost of the event.

Those same three angels visited me in a dream many years later when I was pregnant with my first child. I had a vivid dream that I was baking an elaborate birthday cake when the doorbell rang. Three older ladies stood smiling on my doorstep. They didn't have wings, but I somehow knew they were angels. They instantly made me feel warm and loved. "Sit down," the eldest said. "We have something very important to tell you. Your daughter is coming one week early. But don't worry. Everything is going to be fine and she will be healthy." When I awoke from the dream, I called my sister to compare notes and found that our three angels appeared to be the same. My daughter was born the following Sunday, exactly one week early.

People have also reported happy dream premonitions about love, healings, and even lottery wins. In 2018, *Huff-Post* wrote about a Virginia man who won the lottery after playing numbers that came to him in a dream. He told news reporters that he had never had a dream like that before. The Virginia Lottery Commission said that the odds of his winning were 1 in 278,256. Deng Pravatoudom told

*People Magazine* that her husband dreamed of winning lottery numbers almost two decades before. She played them religiously each year. Then in 2020, after losing her job to the pandemic, she prayed as she played her husband's dream numbers one more time and won. In 1922, Oscar-winning screenwriter T. E. B. Clarke dreamed that a horse named Manna would win the Kentucky Derby. Two years later, he saw an article about a horse named Manna preparing to race in the Derby. He bet two weeks salary and won at odds of 9:1.

L. W. Roger, in his book *Dreams and Premonitions*, recounts several stories of positive premonitions. In a story originally printed in *New York World* in 1908, he tells of a family finding buried treasure thanks to a dream. Lucy Alvord knew that her grandfather had been a prospector. There were rumors in the family that he had found gold and hidden it in the house. But in the seventy years since his passing, no one could find the treasure. Then one night, Lucy dreamed that her grandfather appeared in her bedroom and motioned her to follow him. He took her into the kitchen, where he opened an iron door tucked inside the large oven and pulled out a stone jar filled with gold pieces. The next morning, Lucy asked her brother to break down a wall that covered where the original oven had been. There she found the iron door and a jar filled with gold.

Roger also recounts the story of a widow who believed that when her husband died, he'd left her $5,000. When she went to the bank, however, she learned that he'd withdrawn all the money months before. She had no idea where the money had gone. She was left destitute and was forced to move in with family members. Then one night, she dreamed that she was visiting with her deceased husband. He told her that he'd buried the money at their old house near a shed. She traveled to their old home and dug where her husband had told her the money was hidden. She found all $5,000 buried exactly as her dream predicted.

Premonitory dreams have also led to love. One self-employed divorcée who thought she'd never find love again told me that she was working from home and had few opportunities to meet new people. In her email to me, she wrote:

> On-line dating wasn't for me. Then one day I dreamt that a wonderful man moved into the townhouse next door. In the dream, I was shaking his hand and meeting his Golden Retriever. The next month, my next-door neighbor put her house up for sale and the new man who moved in is now my fiancé! His Golden Retriever, Rex, is going to be our ring bearer."

How does this happen and what does it mean?

I believe we are all connected. The light force of energy that runs through you also runs through me and everyone else walking on this planet. And the ripple effects of this energy can spread far. People who are open to receiving this energy are more susceptible to having dreams that contain premonitions. If you'd like to increase your likelihood of having an intuitive experience, keep your heart open, connect to a source of spirituality, and take time every day to tune in and listen to the heartbeat of the world around you.

**Exercise: Meditation to Visit the Future**

To prime your unconscious mind to receive messages in the dream state, try this meditation each night for about two weeks. In it, you're guided to step into a boat that will take you to the future.

Think of an issue in your life that you'd like to know more about. Write it down on a piece of paper and tuck it under your pillow. For example, you could write: "When will I find a new job?" Or "I will dream about my future love." Try recording this meditation and fall asleep listening to the sound of your voice. Repeat to yourself throughout the day: "I will remember my dreams."

Close your eyes and breathe in deep, full breaths. Allow your body to relax and let go of any tension, stress, or anxiety. As you breathe in, feel your body filling with peace and relaxation. As you breathe out, feel your muscles, tissues, and cells releasing and letting go. Visualize yourself standing on a dock. See the blue sky above you. Hear the seagulls gently calling in the distance. Feel the ocean breeze on your skin. Breathe in the calming sea aromas as the waves lap gently against the dock under your feet.

In the distance, you see a boat coming toward you. Silently call this boat toward you as you focus on your question. As the boat draws near, you see a ramp extend from its side that allows you to step effortlessly onboard.

You feel relaxed and hopeful, knowing that this ship is taking you to a place in the near future.

Visualize yourself standing on the deck of the boat and watch as the shore recedes farther from view. Continue breathing deeply as you mentally focus on your question, knowing the boat will take you to a point in your future.

Soon, the boat stops at another dock. As the ramp extends once more, allowing you to disembark safely, you feel excited knowing that you will soon see a glimpse of your future. As you walk off the boat, you see an empty outdoor movie theater. Sit down in one of the seats and watch as a scene from your future life begins to play out. You may see an image, a color, an individual, or a message displayed on the screen. Try not to force an image to appear. Wait calmly and allow the vision to materialize for you.

When you feel as if you've received the answer you sought, visualize yourself leaving the outdoor theater and walking over to the dock. Climb back onto the boat and see yourself drifting calmly down the smooth sea, returning to where you started. As you walk off the boat back onto the dock, repeat to yourself: "I will receive further insight in my dreams. I will remember my dreams upon waking." Then allow yourself to drift off to sleep.

# Chapter 3

# DREAM VISITATIONS

*Every so often your loved ones will open the door from Heaven and visit you in a dream just to say hello and remind you they are still with you, just in a different way.*

Matt Fraser

Wouldn't it be wonderful if our loved ones could send us postcards from heaven? Imagine how different our grief would be if we knew—beyond a shadow of a doubt—that our loved ones in heaven had arrived safely and were doing just fine. Pharmacologist Julie Beischel, founder of the Windbridge Research Center, has spent years studying mediums. Her research has shown that, when a grieving person sees a therapist in tandem with a medium, the heaviness of the individual's grief subsides greatly. She calls mediums "grief relief tools."

While I agree with and support Beischel's findings, there is nothing as tangible and healing as having your own experience with a departed loved one. It can be incredibly helpful, for example, to hear a medium tell you a nickname that only your loved one knew you were called. But what if you could actually talk to your departed loved ones in your dreams and reach out and hold their hands once more? The impact of these personal dream visits has been shown to be incredibly healing.

Stories abound throughout the centuries of people who've had these dream encounters. Some say that all of these dreams are just the unconscious wish for a reunion with our departed loved ones. But I don't think so. And luckily, my research and personal experience have shown that we can have these dream visits with our own loved ones in heaven.

## KNOCKING ON HEAVEN'S DOOR

The belief in our ability to visit the departed in dreams goes back thousands of years. Plato called our dream time the *metaxus*—a state between worlds. He believed that there is a place we go to in our sleep state where we can meet with ascended beings and our deceased loved ones. First-century BCE writer Cicero told of a man named Simonides who offered to help give a proper burial to a stranger. As Simonides was preparing to sail away on a trip, the stranger he had helped weeks before appeared to him in a dream and warned him not to go. Simonides heeded the warning and later learned that the ship sank and everyone aboard drowned. Saint Ambrose likewise wrote about two deceased saints, Gervasius and Protasius, who appeared to him in a dream to offer advice.

Many lucky people experience frequent dream visits with their loved ones. When Jamie Fox accepted his Oscar, he thanked his grandmother for being his first teacher. Then he added: "Now she talks to me in my dreams. And I can't wait to go to sleep tonight because we've got a lot to talk about." But experience has taught me that loved ones in heaven often need permission from higher beings and must have a very good reason to enter our dreams. If they were able to visit us in dreams every night, we might never work through our grief and learn to move on.

In Robert Moss's book *The Dreamer's Book of the Dead*, he recounts the story of a friend who dreamed that her mother was carrying huge buckets. When she asked why, her mother said: "These buckets contain the weight of your tears. You are constantly filling them up by grieving for me. Until you release the grief, I can't move on." The weight of our grief can actually keep our loved ones from doing the work they need to do on the other side. Still, when we need them, the dead can appear in our dreams to say a final goodbye, to impart an important message, to offer guidance or warnings, and to help with unfinished business.

Perhaps the most important characteristic of these dream visits is that, in them, our deceased loved ones generally appear to be healthy and happy. In the majority of cases, they look the same as they did when they were alive and in their prime. Before my mother-in-law passed away, she had lost a leg due to diabetic complications. But when she appears in my dreams, she looks the way she did the first year I met her. In fact, in her first dream appearance, she hopped on each leg and said: "Look! I've got two good legs again!"

However, sometimes our loved ones show up looking just as they did the day they died. When a friend's father died, within days she had a dream in which he appeared at the foot of her bed to say a final goodbye. "He did not look good at all," she told me. "He looked just as tired and worn out as he did the day he left us. When I told him he didn't look like himself, a light fell over him and he appeared just as he looked when I was a little girl."

In my years of encountering spirits in dreams and doing readings for clients, I've learned that our loved ones have to learn how to manipulate their energy in order to appear in our dreams. I did a reading for a woman who had recently lost her husband. He kept saying: "Tell her I'm trying to come through in her dreams, but I can't learn how to use my energy. Please tell her I'm sorry about the dream." When I recounted this message to my client, she rolled her eyes and said: "He should be sorry! That scared the shit out of me!"

I couldn't help but laugh a little at her outburst and asked her to explain. She said she woke up one night about six months after her husband passed away. She knew she was dreaming, but she was sitting up in her actual bed looking out into the hallway. Then she saw her husband walking toward her. "Except his skin kept falling off. It scared the life out of me." That's when I learned that, since spirits don't have bodies, they have to learn how to re-create their forms when they appear in our dreams. This apparently takes a lot of trial and error.

My best friend died at only twenty-seven from colon cancer. He appeared to me in a dream five years later in which he was sitting outside a restaurant we used to frequent. As I approached him and realized who he was, I became so excited that I rushed over to hug him. But he stopped me and said: "I can't do that yet. I haven't taken the class on how to use my energy for physical contact. But just sit next to me and we can catch up." He then explained that he has to learn how to work with the forces of energy to connect with me in the dream state.

These stories demonstrate how hard our loved ones try to reach us from beyond the veil. They want to connect with us as much as we want to hear from them. The timing of these dream visits varies from person to person, however. If you've lost loved ones and haven't had a dream visit with them, be patient. It can take a lot of time, because they have to get acclimated to their new surroundings first. Then they have to learn how to work with both their energy and yours to enter your dream state.

## THE GREAT BARRIER GRIEF

Your own personal grief can act as a barrier that pushes the energy of the deceased away and keeps them from connecting with you in your dreams. If you're still actively grieving, but want to hear from a loved one, before falling asleep say to him or her: "I give you permission to enter my dreams. If you can't, please try to visit someone close to both of us in their dreams, so I can still hear from you." It's often much easier for our deceased loved ones to enter the dream state of a close family friend, because that friend may not be grieving with the same intensity.

One friend of mine dreamed that her next-door neighbor's recently deceased husband was walking by the house. He waved to her and said: "Tell my wife I made it. Love you, Tweetie!" When my friend walked next door and relayed the dream to the new widow, the woman collapsed in tears, saying that Tweetie was his special nickname for her because she was so chatty.

It is often easier for our loved ones to appear in a dream to someone who isn't grieving. One evening before a full day of readings, I had an intense and vivid dream that I was walking past a row of bleachers at a college football game. I could smell the crisp, clean fall air. I heard the marching band gearing up for the half-time show. As I scanned the students in the bleachers, I noticed a young man standing up and waving to me frantically. When I approached him, he held out a hunter-green sweatshirt with the college logo on it and said: "Tell my mom I made it! I'm in heaven and going to college here. I met a great girl too. Tell her I'm sorry for leaving, but I am happy now."

When my third client of the day entered my office, I knew she was the mother for whom that dream was intended. When I recounted the dream to her, she started to cry and said: "I still have his hunter-green sweatshirt. He never got to wear it because he passed away the summer after his high school graduation. But I'm happy to know he's attending college in heaven."

When one client came to see me, she was clearly in deep mourning. Her husband had passed away unexpectedly in his sleep just two years after their wedding. She vowed to remain single until they met again on the other side. His main message in the reading was his desire to see her happily married again, but she was not ready to hear this. I didn't push the husband's message because I know that processing grief takes time. We all must learn to carry it in our own way. My client emailed me a year later:

> Samantha, thank you for the reading you did for me last June. When we met, I wasn't ready to hear the messages my husband was trying to share. But about six months later, I had this vivid dream that I was driving with my husband. It felt like an ordinary Saturday like we used to share just running errands. He was driving and kept repeating: "Say yes to Anthony. You'll be happy, and it makes me happy to see you happy. Say yes to Anthony." I had no idea what this dream meant, but it felt so real! I didn't know an Anthony.
>
> But just a few weeks after that dream, we hired a consultant at work. His name is Anthony, and we've been dating for two months now. I still feel a little guilty finding happiness with someone new, but then I think of that dream and I am reassured.

This is what our loved ones on the other side want for us—our happiness. While our love does go on and we can continue to honor, love, and miss our family and friends in heaven, they are aware that this life is for the living. They want nothing more than to see us happy and will often come in dreams to convey this message. But they can't just pop in for a dream visit anytime they (or you) want to reconnect, because this would hamper our own ability to process our grief. If you could connect with your loved ones every night in your dreams, you'd risk staying in the early stages of grief and never come out the other side.

## MESSAGES FROM BEYOND

Another characteristic of dream visits is that they are organized and realistic, and usually convey a message. Traditional dreams are often random, make little to no sense, and feel like something out of *Alice in Wonderland*. By contrast, dream encounters from loved ones in heaven feel like actual visits. The dream often occurs in the home you shared or in a place you both loved to visit. The dream experience progresses in a realistic, chronological fashion. These dreams have a sense of reality and familiarity to them and feel like an actual reunion with your loved one.

After one friend's mom passed away, she dreamed that she was walking down a trail behind her childhood home when her mother suddenly appeared and joined her on her walk. They talked over the last few weeks and discussed the funeral, joking about the minister mispronouncing their last name. Her mom thanked her for following her wishes and giving her a beautiful send off. When they reached the end of the trail, her mother said: "Well, looks like it's time to say goodbye. I love you honey and I'm always here for you." And then my friend woke up. The dream felt so real to her that she swears that, upon waking, she could smell her mother's perfume lingering in the bedroom.

It takes a considerable amount of energy for our deceased loved ones to enter our dreams, so they usually only make the effort when it's needed. And I've repeatedly been told that they have to receive permission from their guides and yours in order to do so. They must have a reason, a purpose, for meeting you in the dream state. We exist here under the law of free will. If our loved ones could drop in for a dream visit just to offer advice or guidance, it could impact our own ability to make decisions. So dream visits typically occur to deliver an important message or request. They may also offer a chance for one final goodbye or an opportunity to share important information.

Over a decade ago, I dreamed that I was awakened by a loud crash in my living room. When I rushed to investigate, I found my mother-in-law on the floor. "I don't have much time," she said. "I can already feel my energy fading, so listen to me. You're going to be fine. Okay? You're going to be just fine. It's nothing. Oh—and tell Grace congratulations." Then I woke up back in my bed.

I stared up at the ceiling for a long time trying to make sense of this message. I was doing just fine in life and had no serious issues to worry about. And why had she mentioned my husband's niece? I woke up my husband and told him about the dream. He called his sister and told her about my dream. When he hung up the phone, he turned to me and said: "I don't think that was just a dream. Last night, Grace found out she made the junior Olympics ski team."

All day long, I was haunted by that dream. What was it that I didn't have to worry about? That night, after I put my children to bed, I hopped in the shower, and that's when I found the answer. I discovered a lump in my right breast. It was cancerous, but I caught it early. I'm grateful to say that, after a mastectomy, I have been cancer free for ten years.

Loved ones also appear in our dreams to pass on requests. One of my clients had a dream shortly after his aunt passed away. In the dream, she was in her home pacing back and forth, wringing her hands in distress. When he asked her what was wrong, she told him that there was another insurance policy that her husband didn't know about. When my client called his uncle, they were able to track down a sizeable insurance policy his aunt had neglected to tell anyone about.

## RESCUE ME!

Dream visits often occur during times of stress, or to offer help and comfort during an unhappy or chaotic time in our lives. Loved ones will often journey from heaven to our dreams during periods of great upheaval, just as they would move mountains here on Earth if they were still physically with us. Imagine that you're living in America and your brother moves to New Zealand. If your brother were going through a stressful time, you'd spend thousands of dollars to make the sixteen-hour flight to be by his side. But would you invest this time and money to visit him if he were not somehow at risk? Probably not.

The same logic applies to dream visits from our loved ones on the other side. Obviously it doesn't cost them money to visit us, but they do have to invest a considerable amount of energy in the visit and must obtain permission from guides and angels. When we need to hear from them, however, they show up for us.

Keep in mind that most of us only remember a few dreams a week. But your loved ones can visit you from heaven at any time, and you may not be consciously aware of these visits. A listener to my podcast emailed me this story:

> I love listening to your dream stories on the show and wanted to share my own. When I first started hearing about all your dream experiences, I'm not gonna lie, I was little envious. I was very close to my grandfather. My dad left shortly after I was born and mom and I lived with my grandparents. So Pops was more like a dad to me. After he died, I kept waiting for him to show up in a dream, but he never did. After listening to your recent episode on soul travels, I went to bed that night kind of yelling at my Pops and said: "Why can't you appear in my dreams too?" Nothing happened that night.
>
> Throughout that month, my life started to unravel. My company laid me off, and the following week, my doctor found polyps on my thyroid. The night before the biopsy, I dreamt

that Pops was in my room. He was surrounded by this brilliant light that lit up my whole room. I knew I was awake, but I knew I was sleeping. In the dream, I couldn't move or speak. Pops said to me: "I've visited you in your dreams plenty of times, but your mind is busier than a hamster on a wheel so you tend to forget. I'm always here for you. That will never change. Sure, everything feels messy now but just you wait. In a few days, good news is coming." As he and the light faded, I heard him whistling the song "My Girl."

When I woke up, I thought about all the mornings I'd started the day humming the lyrics to that song. Pops used to sing me that song, but I always assumed I woke up with that on my mind because I was missing him. Now I guess he was visiting me all those times because the biopsy showed that there was nothing wrong with my thyroid. Oh and I just started a really great new job with even better benefits!

Our loved ones want to share messages of comfort, love, and support. We just have to be quiet and listen.

Three weeks before one client was getting married, her future father-in-law had a sudden heart attack and died. She and her fiancé wanted to cancel the wedding because they didn't feel right going through with it so soon after his passing, even though it meant that they would lose a lot of money. The day they decided to call it off, my client had a dream in which she was sitting in a pew in a small church with her fiancé's dad sitting next to her. A man and woman stood at the altar before a minister holding a Bible while a small, elderly lady played an old, out-of-tune piano.

"This was my wedding," he said. "It was just Jane and me. Her parents didn't approve of me, so we didn't have the big wedding she had always wanted. I didn't care. I just wanted to marry Jane, but I knew it bugged her that she never got her big day. And it will bug me too if you don't get your big day." Later that morning, her future mother-in-law called to tell her that, when she walked through the living room that morning, she found her wedding photo had fallen off the wall. "I think it's a sign from Jimmy," she said. "I think he wants you to go ahead with the wedding." The big day went forward as planned.

## MAN'S BEST FRIEND

In *A Study Examining Dreams in the Healing Process Through Dreams in Bereavement,* researchers revealed that animals are often present in dreams that occur in the early stages of grief. They concluded that the presence of animals in these dreams tends to alleviate anxiety for the dreamer. Further study shows that, as the dreamer becomes comfortable with the dream visits, the animal companions no longer appear. I believe, however, that our deceased pets make their presence known in our dreams for the same reasons that our friends and family traverse the veil to visit us. They want us to know that they are happy, safe, and grateful for the love and support they shared with us on their earthly journey.

Many traditional religions claim that animals don't have souls. Yet many people report dreaming of their deceased animals returning to them to say hello, to offer comfort, or to share important messages. When one of my clients lost her beloved French bulldog, she was distraught. Months later, she considered getting another puppy, but decided against it, feeling it would be a betrayal of her pet's memory. Then one night, she had a dream that she was waiting outside on an airport tarmac watching a plane descend. Her deceased pet got off the plane with a new puppy trailing after her. When she woke up, she had no idea what the dream meant. Then she received an email telling her that one of her dog's litter mates had given birth to puppies and asking if she would be interested in adopting one. The only hitch was that the family had moved to Texas, so the new puppy would have to arrive by airplane. My client took her dream as confirmation and said yes to the new puppy.

My family and I adopted a doberman named Gretchen who'd been rescued from a breeding facility. When she joined our family, Gretchen quickly bonded with us. Years later, when she passed from old age, I heard her paws running through the house late at night just as she used to do when she was alive, checking to see that we were all safe in our beds before falling asleep. This went on for about a week after she died, and I prayed that she would feel safe enough to leave us and go into the light

Then one night, I had a dream that I was standing atop a large mountain with Gretchen by my side. I knelt down and told her: "Thank you for being such an important member of our family. Your work is done here. You can still check on us, but first you must go through the light." She licked my hand and rested her head against me. I awoke soon after, and now I no longer hear her ghostly jaunt through the house. Sometimes pets, just like people, need a little nudge to pass over into the light.

Animals can also appear in our dreams as guides. When a friend of mine started practicing out-of-body journeying when he slept, he often dreamed of a wolf standing guard next to him. He believes the wolf keeps him safe while his soul travels at night. My daughter often has wonderful dreams in which an owl is present. We were walking through a farmer's market when she told me about these dreams. "Do you think the owl is some kind of guide for me?" she asked. Just then, we came upon a table sponsored by our local exotic-bird rescue group. They had their pet owl with them. "I think that's your answer," I said.

I received an email from a podcast listener who shared a dream she experienced after the painful, sudden loss of her cat.

> When my cat became ill suddenly and had to
> be put down, I was a mass of sadness and guilt.
> I wasn't sure if I'd done the right thing. Should
> I have insisted on more tests? Why didn't I get a
> second opinion? Each night, I prayed that Milly
> was okay and that she forgave me. Then last
> night, I had a dream that I woke up in my bed.
> Milly jumped on the bed and lay down next to
> me just as she had every night of her life. Next to

my bed was a clock radio (that isn't there in my real bedroom). It suddenly turned on and began playing Bob Marley's "Everything's Gonna Be Alright." In the dream, I just sat there with Milly stroking her silky black ears as I listened to the lyrics. I really feel it was my Milly visiting me to tell me she was okay with her passing and happy on the other side.

## KEEPING THE DOOR OPEN

If we remain open to the concept that our loved ones can visit us in our dreams, then we can open our energy and consciousness to receive more of these dream visits and obtain the comfort they're meant to provide. In *Dreamwork for the Soul*, Rosemary Ellen Guiley, a leading expert in the metaphysical and paranormal fields, writes: "The land of dreams is part of the *mundus imaginalis*, or imaginal world, a real place recognized by cultures around the world since ancient times." We can access this liminal world through petition, meditation, and dreams. Major religions through-out the world and across time have tended to condemn this type of communication with deceased loved ones because it goes against dogma. If our loved ones survive death and aren't sleeping in their graves or hanging out in purgatory awaiting resurrection, then what does that mean for their doctrines?

But people continue to have these experiences with their loved ones in dreams. A study published in the journal

*Dreaming* evaluated 268 dreamers who had recently lost a close loved one. They also looked at 162 volunteers who had recently lost a beloved pet. More than 80 percent of the volunteers reported having a dream visit from a loved one in heaven, while more than 77 percent had a dream about a deceased pet. The study also revealed that people who tend to remember their dreams in general report having more of these dream visits compared to those who typically don't recall their dreams. In chapter 11, I'll give you some tips on how to remember your dreams more vividly.

Many believe that, when we dream of our loved ones, it's not us reaching out to them in grief, but rather them soliciting us in their own dream time on the other side. Robert Moss writes:

> An element that is usually lacking in modern discussions of dream visitation by the dead is the possibility that the dead are dreaming of us. My friend Elizabeth dreamt she met Dorothy Parker—famous as the mordant wit of the Algonquin Round Table in the 1920s—and asked whether she ever attended séances when she was alive. Dorothy Parker flashed back, faster than you could pluck an olive from a martini: "I'm holding one now. How you do you think you got to meet me?" The poet and spiritual writer William Butler Yeats called this "dreaming back" and theorized that the dead call us to visit them in the dream state. (*Dreamers Book of the Dead*)

William Thomas Stead, once called "the most famous journalist in the British Empire," was also a well-known Spiritualist who even channeled a book through his daughter about the other side after his tragic death on the *Titanic*. He believed that everyone should reach out to their departed loved ones, either through dreams or meditation. Moss quotes him as saying: "It's not only possible and lawful, but an absolute duty on the part of mortals to keep up a loving intercourse with the loved ones who've gone before us."

To maintain this "loving intercourse" and solicit dreams with your loved ones in heaven, talk about them throughout the day. Share their stories. Keep a photo of them by your bedside. As you fall asleep, mentally ask them to visit you in your dreams. The exercise below can help you initiate contact with your loved ones tonight.

**Exercise: Hello From Heaven**
Before going to sleep, write a letter to your loved ones in heaven. Tell them everything you've wanted to share with them since they passed. Ask them to appear to you in a dream. If you're still in the grieving process, it can be difficult energetically for a loved one to get through your grief to enter your dreams, because grief acts like a barrier around your aura. If that is the case, ask your loved one to appear to a close friend or family member in a dream to bring a message through to you. Consider placing a photo of the person next to your bed.

As you're falling asleep, think of happy memories of your loved ones while repeating to yourself: "I will remember my dreams tonight." Tuck the letter under your pillow.

You can also place a small tumbled amethyst, unakite, lapis lazuli, or moonstone under your pillow as well. These crystals are known to help us recall our dreams.

In the morning, don't move. Resist jumping out of bed and starting your day. Simply lie there and travel back in your mind to recall any dreams you've just experienced. Even if you recall just an image or a color, write this down. Studies have shown that the more we record our dreams, the more fully we will begin to remember our nighttime soul travels.

# Chapter 4

# GHOSTS AND
# LOVED ONES

*It's not an easy thing, living in two worlds at the same time.*

Robert Moss

We are born with free will and we die with free will. This means that, if souls choose not to pass into the light, they have the free will to remain ghosts. There are many reasons why someone might choose this fate. If their religious beliefs have taught them that suicides go to hell, yet the pain of living on Earth led them to take their own lives, they may choose to remain ghosts. Some souls choose to remain earthbound because they'd rather stay and wait for a loved one to cross with them. Those who are murdered may want to see their killers brought to justice, so they refuse the light and stay on Earth.

I've encountered ghosts who won't cross over for a variety of reasons. One woman who was haunting a home told me she refused to cross over because she didn't want to spend eternity with her husband. Another ghost who was haunting the office where I worked revealed that her son went missing in Vietnam. She refused to cross over until she knew where he was. The ghosts I've encountered tend to be newer souls or people who just refuse to evolve and grow. They tend to be stuck in their ways and very rigid in their beliefs. As poet, novelist, and critic Andrew Lang once said: "Since the days of Ancient Egypt, ghosts have learned, and forgotten, nothing."

One of the earliest recorded ghost stories centers on a woman named Philinnion who lived during the fourth century BCE. She died six months after her arranged marriage to a general in Alexander the Great's army. Soon after her death, she began appearing in her parents' home. They had a handsome guest staying with them named Machates with whom, according to the ancient writers, she began an intimate, ghostly relationship. When they were discovered by one of the household staff, she defended herself by saying that her affair was approved by the gods of the underworld. Her parents, worried that she was someone else from the underworld masquerading as their daughter, had her tomb opened only to discover that her body was missing. Then Machates, the ghost's young lover, showed the parents pieces of jewelry he had received from her as gifts. The pieces had been buried her with and were also missing from the tomb.

In the first century, Plutarch wrote about a Spartan general named Pausanias who died around 470 BCE. When Pausanias was at the height of his career, he called a young Byzantine woman named Cleonice to his room one evening and tried to force himself upon her. When she refused, he murdered her. Cleonice then became a *ker*—a tormenting spirit—and haunted Pausanias in his dreams, appearing to him as a ghost who cried out: "Draw thou nigh to thy doom; 'tis evil for men to be wanton." Consumed with fear and guilt, Pausanias consulted the oracle at Heraclea. Through the oracle, Cleonice told him that she'd stop haunting him if he returned to Sparta. Pausanias was arrested as a traitor upon his return to Sparta and was condemned to death by starvation. He was walled up in Athena's temple. After he died, he too became a ker and mediums had to be called in to exorcize his spirit.

A spirit is someone who has passed through the light and crossed over to the other side. A ghost, on the other hand, is someone who has refused to go into the light and remains bound to the Earth. Ghosts often need the help of mediums to cross over successfully. And sometimes spirits also need our earthly assistance. Even though spirits have successfully crossed into the light, they often still need our help and prayers, because there's still so much work for them to do on the other side. They have to go through a life review, look at their soul's plan, and evaluate how well they did. And they need to go through their own grieving process just as much as we grieve when we lose them. Finally, they are often encouraged to return to Earth so they can further evolve their souls. All of this takes time and energy, and often requires our assistance.

# HELPING SPIRITS CROSS OVER

Just as our departed loved ones can appear in our dreams to offer guidance, confirmation, and affirming messages, we are often called upon as soul travelers to help them as well. Stories have surfaced throughout history of ghosts and spirits reaching out to us in the dream state to request our help.

Those of us who are open to helping souls in the dream state can perform a wonderful service to the newly departed, who may find themselves stuck in their own grieving process or resistant to giving up their beliefs. Dream writer and teacher Robert Moss maintains:

> The dead come calling in our dreams because they need help or guidance from us—often because they are lost or lonely or stuck somewhere not very far away. There are guides available on the other side, of course, but the dead may have remained so physically oriented, so enmeshed in their dense energy bodies, that they are inclined to trust someone who has a physical body more than a being who does not. (*Dreamers' Book of the Dead*)

When I was going through my own spiritual awakening, my dream life evolved into a powerful nightly tour of the other side.

One night, I dreamed that I was awakened in my bed by a friendly, older gentleman. I remember sitting up in the dream and staring at him. He was wearing faded blue jeans and a denim shirt, and had on an old red baseball cap covering a head of thick, gray hair. He introduced himself as Red and shook my hand. I nodded and tried to smile, but I couldn't seem to find my voice in this dream. Red asked me to follow him into the kitchen, which I found was full of people. Red stayed by my side and kept a fatherly, calm hand on my back. "Go on darlin," he said. "They just want to talk to you."

I walked up to a woman who looked to be in her mid-fifties with short, gray hair and a strong, comforting presence. "Hold my hand," she said. "I want to show you something." Her cocoa-colored hand was warm and I was instantly transported to a car in a parking lot. I looked around me and saw ambulances and a hospital sign. I was in a small Honda hatchback with the woman seated in the driver's seat wearing a nurse's uniform. Suddenly, she was gripped by a scorching pain in her chest and I watched helplessly as she bent over, opened the driver's door, and fell to the ground. In the next moment, I was back in my kitchen holding her hand. She gave me a wry smile and said: "It was a Monday when I died."

I spent the rest of the dream greeting everyone in my kitchen, holding their hands and witnessing their last moments on Earth. One man died sitting on a tractor in the fields of his farm. Another had been killed in a car accident. They all seemed to die quickly and unexpectedly. I don't know why it was so important for me to witness these last moments with them, but I was honored to be part of it. I felt as if my sitting with them during their last moments in my dream helped them to cross over to the other side fully.

After I had greeted everyone in my kitchen, Red walked me back to bed and tucked me in. He pulled the blankets over me and patted my hand, then sat on the edge of the bed and said: "Now was that so bad?" I shook my head, apparently still unable to find my voice. "We've been trying to come to you for years," he said. "Finally I came up with this idea. It's not so scary in a dream, is it?" I nodded in agreement.

After that, I started having many dreams in which people just wanted to show me how they had died. In one, I was seated at a huge mahogany dining room table with a family of twelve. I patiently "witnessed" all their last moments on Earth. I've had many dreams where I'm seated at an outdoor café by the ocean. In these dreams, there's always a long line of people waiting to sit down and talk to me. All they want to do is tell me how they died.

Since death is so final and traumatic, I feel that mediums like myself can act as a link between this side and the next, helping the newly deceased process the trauma of this final, permanent change in their soul's journey. In many of my soul travels, I am helping the newly deceased recognize that they are now dead and that they need to go through the light to the other side.

In one vivid dream, I was standing on the side of a highway with two young people in front of me. I knew they were siblings and I also knew they had just died in the car crash I could see behind them. I tried to get them to acknowledge what had happened to them, but couldn't seem to get through to them. Then I became aware of someone, a presence, behind me that said: "This isn't working.

We have to take them up directly." As I watched, the two were pulled up in a white tube of energy.

Another night, I dreamed I was standing outside a hospital with a young girl who looked to be about nine or ten. She was in a hospital gown holding a teddy bear, peering past me and watching as cars picked up or dropped off patients. When I told her she needed to go through the light, she didn't answer me. Again I felt a presence behind me who told me to encourage the girl to look into the light, where she'd see her family.

"If you peer into that light, you'll see your grandmother. She's waiting for you," I said. The girl stopped trying to look around me and finally spoke. "I'm waiting for my parents," she said. "They're supposed to pick me up." My heart went out to her.

"No," I said quietly, gently. "You're meant to pass on now and go to heaven. You're going to have so much fun there. And you can pop in and visit your parents whenever you like. Anytime. But you can't do that until you go through the light." Prompted by the presence behind me, I sent a mental message to the child's grandmother and watched as her hand reached out through the tunnel of light. The little girl looked up at me and I nodded. She tucked her teddy bear under her arm and, with her other hand, reached for her grandmother. I peered into the tunnel and watched as the two embraced and then walked into the light together. As I stood there by myself in front of the hospital, I heard the presence behind me say: "Well done."

The little girl had apparently been waiting for years for her parents to pick her up from the hospital. This made me wonder whether time stands still for ghosts. Are they in a dimension we just can't understand, or are they stuck in this movie called life that's been temporarily paused for them? I don't know. But it did comfort me to learn that the child's guides had been with her all this time trying to help her cross. Why was I able to do it now? Perhaps because she was finally ready.

Even when spirits are ready to cross over to the other side, however, there are still many choices they often need help with. Recently, I dreamed that I was assisting a young girl who had just gotten to heaven. We were standing in a lush, beautiful garden with three paths in front of us. The path on the left would return her to a new life on Earth. The middle path would allow her to visit happy memories from the life she'd just left. The third path would allow her to move on to the next level of heaven. She wanted to return to her old life. I gently told her that this wasn't possible. I knew it was my job to get her to walk down the path of memories so she could find the inner courage and resolution to move on to the next level of heaven. When I showed her how to walk down this path, she was relieved and happy.

Each year, as I learn more and more about this strange, wonderful world we live in, I realize there is so little I truly understand. But I have learned that we soul travelers can help these in-between souls recognize where they are now and, more important, where they need to go. I've also learned that souls who are temporarily stuck are never alone. I knew in each of these dream experiences that their guides and angels were with these souls the whole time.

They just couldn't see them. And that's where soul travelers come in. People who are intuitive, open, and able to provide this service can act as a link between this world and the next.

## GHOSTLY ENCOUNTERS

Many people think it's cool or interesting to have a ghost in their home. I disagree. When we're alive, we get our energy from food and water. When we cross over, we receive our energy from the light. But for those who choose to remain between the two worlds, they have to get their energy from us. Ghosts in your home will take your energy. They may not do it intentioanlly, but they create an energy drain nonetheless. Car keys may go missing just as you're about to leave the house. You rush around searching for them, only to discover that they're exactly where you looked at first. In your rushing around, your aura emits a burst of stressful energy that can "feed" the ghost and fuel it with needed energy.

Ghosts often appear in our dreams to request or offer help. In *A Christmas Carol*, Jacob Marley appears in Scrooge's dream to prepare him for the night ahead, but also to act as a warning. He's trying to help Scrooge avoid his own miserable fate. In Shakespeare's *Richard III*, the ghosts of his victims appear in Richard's dreams to warn of his upcoming defeat, leaving him to lament: "I did but dream. O coward conscious, how dost thou afflict me."

In my hometown, there's a well-documented story of a ghost appearing in the dreams of a friend asking for help.

One winter evening in 1810, Samuel Joselyn was visiting a hunting lodge with his wife. The two argued and Joselyn got on his horse to ride away through the dark swamp. When his horse returned without him, a search party was dispatched to locate him. His body was discovered in four inches of freezing water. It's believed he either fell or was thrown from his horse.

For the next three days, Joselyn's ghost appeared in the dreams of his closest friend, Sandy Hostler. In each dream, Joselyn told his friend that he was buried alive and to please come and save him. After the third night, Sandy reached out to a mutual friend who reminded him of a pact the three friends had made years earlier. They agreed that whoever died first would return from the dead to confirm an afterlife. They went to see Joselyn's parents to recount the harrowing dream visits. Joselyn's father, a respected local attorney, immediately arranged for a group of men to meet at the graveyard where his son was buried to exhume his body. To their horror and dismay, they discovered that the inside of the coffin lid was covered in bloody scratches and his fingers were torn nearly to the bone. The coroner later confirmed that Joselyn had been buried alive.

Ghosts have also appeared in dreams to help solve their own murders. In 1977, firefighters were called to the home of Teresita Basa in Chicago. After putting out the fire, they discovered that she'd been stabbed to death. Basa had arrived in this country from the Philippines and had lived a quiet life of service as a respiratory therapist. Police could find no motive for the crime. Everyone had loved her. Because of the fire, however, forensic evidence yielded few results.

Five months later, Basa's co-worker, Remibias Chua, who was also originally from the Philippines, began having dreams in which her co-worker appeared to her begging for help in catching her murderer. One afternoon, while Chua was napping, her husband said that she began speaking in a different voice that claimed to be Basa. The voice said that a co-worker named Allan Showery had killed her. When Chua awoke, she had no memory of a voice speaking through her.

This bizarre episode then happened a second time. Basa spoke through Chua while she was sleeping and asked her husband why they hadn't gone to the police. He explained that they had no evidence to bring to the police other than these strange dreams. Basa, still speaking through a sleeping Chua, told him that the murderer had taken her jewelry and given it to his girlfriend. Finally, the couple went to the police.

When detectives did a background check on Showery, co-workers revealed that he had told them he was going to Basa's home the night of the murder to fix her TV. When they contacted Showery's girlfriend and asked if he had given her any jewelry, she confirmed that he had and agreed to let them show it to Basa's family, who identified it as their daughter's. When confronted with this evidence, Showery confessed and was imprisoned for murder.

How could Teresita Basa have been able to connect with her co-worker? Perhaps the link was their shared home country. In Joselyn's case, he was able to appear in Hostler's dream because they shared a bond of friendship. Once there's an emotional link between two people, that link survives death. It may be that a shared background and mutual workplace linked Teresita Basa and Remibias Chua in a similar way.

Many mystics, clairvoyants, and healers write about energy cords that connect us to each other. Like an umbilical cord that links a mother and child, these cords exchange energy, thoughts, and emotions. These cords are created whenever there's a bond of friendship or love, supporting an exchange of energy between two people. Have you ever randomly thought of someone and then heard from that person the next day? When you thought about this person, you unconsciously tugged on that energy cord. The other person unconsciously felt it and was inspired to reach out to you.

Even a small exchange of energy can create a cord. You can be connected to co-workers, to neighbors, or even to the bagger at your grocery store who always helps you to your car. These cords may not be as strong as others, but they still create an energy link. It may be that Teresita Basa was able to connect with Remibias Chua because they had so much in common. They were both from the Philippines and they worked in healthcare at the same hospital. And I believe Chua must have been energetically open to this exchange—perhaps from a natural intuitive inclination, or a strong compassionate heart, or a meditation practice. Anyone who practices compassion, has empathy for others, and takes time to still their mind through meditation and prayer can serve as a vehicle for these miraculous experiences.

## ASSISTING LOVED ONES
## IN HEAVEN

Often our loved ones reach out to us asking for help from the other side. More than twenty years after my maternal grandmother died, I had a series of intriguing dream experiences in which she asked for assistance. In the first, I awoke in my bedroom. I knew I was dreaming and I knew I was awake. I later learned that this is called lucid dreaming (see chapter 7). In the dream, I could feel a presence calling me to my living room, where I saw my grandmother. Her skin was sallow, her eyes were sunken in, and she was dressed in a tattered, yellowed shift. She didn't speak to me, but I heard her thoughts. It was as if she were speaking inside my head. She said she was having a hard time on the other side dealing with the residue of regret and asked me to pray for her. I promised I would and awoke the next moment back in my bed.

When I told my mother about the dream, she was understandably very upset and wanted to know why Grammy would still be suffering all these years later. She told me that, soon after my grandmother died, she was plagued with dreams of her mother facing two doors. In the dream, she turned to my mother and said: "I don't want to go through the left door, but they're making me." I explained that the left door most likely led to the life-review process and that sometimes this process can take years. "She must have just finished her life-review process," I said, "and now she needs our prayers to continue her healing." I have no idea how I knew this. The words just tumbled out of my mouth. I've since discovered that soul travelers often receive information subconsciously in dream experiences. To my mother's credit, she never doubted this or me. She called her sisters and her cousin and asked them to pray for Grammy.

Two weeks later, I had another lucid dream. I "awoke" to that feeling of a presence and walked out into the living room where my grandmother awaited me. But this time, she was radiant with light. She was wearing makeup. Her hair was all done up in a French twist and she was wearing a navy Chanel suit—the kind from the 1980s with gold buttons. I remember thinking: "That was the outfit she always wished she could wear." She took my hands and I felt that they were soft and warm. She glowed with an inner light of peace. She smiled and said: "Thank you for the prayers," and then she dissolved into a tube of light. Once again, I woke up back in my bed.

Had my grandmother been in purgatory? I don't know. I'm not sure it's that simple. But I do know that, somehow, all our prayers helped her finally to love herself and to take her rightful place in the light.

When we die, we each undertake a life review in which we experience everything we did—the good and the bad, from our own perspective, as well as from the perspective of the people who were on the receiving end of our actions. Because my grandmother died holding a lot of anger and resentment, she had a hard time going through her life review and most likely kept postponing it. A year after these two dreams, I had another vivid dream in which I was walking by the ocean. I saw my grandmother strolling by with a group of friends, laughing and smiling. I waved to her and she waved back. That was it. We didn't speak, but I believe she appeared in this dream to show me that she was indeed healing and doing very well on the other side.

A listener to my podcast shared a compelling dream she had about helping her own grandmother cross over to the other side.

> Several years ago, the night my grandmother died, I had a dream where she and I were in our beloved family cabin drinking coffee. I looked at her and saw she was crying. I realized in an instant that she had died and was sad to be crossing over and was struggling to let go. Even though my grandmother had lost both of her children and her husband, she loved life and, I think, hung on for longer than she might have because she knew my sister and I needed her as we had already lost our parents.
>
> I went to her and hugged her and told her it was okay to let go and that I knew how hard it was, but my sister and I would be okay. It only took a few moments but she became translucent and began to drift away through my arms, out

the window and toward the lake outside. When I woke up, I had total certainty that she had died. I noticed as I awoke that my thinking brain crept in with doubt, but when I checked my phone I saw the missed call from her nursing home and they confirmed what I already knew. She had passed away that night.

## THE POWER OF PRAYER

Praying for the dead has been a beloved tradition in almost every religion throughout the ages. Buddhists light a candle for their deceased loved ones to help light the way to the other side. Jews observe Yahrtzeit on the anniversary of a loved one's passing. They light candles, share memories, and offer prayers to assist their loved ones in heaven. Catholics have Masses said for their deceased loved ones in which the whole congregation prays for the departed souls.

Studies have documented the very real and positive effect prayer can have on the living. In 1988, cardiologist Randolph Byrd published one of the first major studies on the powerful impact of prayer, investigating 393 patients who were admitted to the hospital for heart attack or chest pain. Those who received prayer had better clinical outcomes than those who did not. When physicians Wayne Jonas and Cindy Crawford examined more than 2,000 published reports on the power of prayer, they concluded: "There is evidence to suggest that mind and matter interact in a way that is consistent with the assumptions of distant healing. Mental intention has effects on non-living random systems and may have effects on living systems." Physician Larry Dossey, in *Healing Words: The Power of Prayer and the Practice of Medicine,* concurs: "If only a single one of these studies is valid, then a nonlocal dimension of consciousness exists."

If what Dossey says is true, then it makes sense that this "nonlocal dimension" may also include the afterlife and that our prayers for the dead can help them. Our loved ones on the other side sometimes need our help and simply praying for them can assist them on their own soul journeys. You can help your loved ones in heaven by telling their stories, placing pictures of them around the house, and praying for them.

Our soul work does not end when we die. Death is more like a graduation. The work of the soul continues and the deceased often need our help in furthering their soul development. You can help your loved ones in heaven by placing a candle in front of a photo or special memento of theirs. Light the candle each day while saying this or a similar prayer:

> I pray that the light of this candle finds you
> in heaven and fills you with all my love. I pray
> and intend that you're continuing to heal and
> grow on the other side. I treasure you and all
> our memories.

Make it a point to celebrate your loved ones' birthdays and anniversaries with joy. I have a friend who still throws her mother a birthday party each year, even though she died seven years ago. She doesn't blow up balloons and invite friends over. But she always cooks a special meal, bakes her mom's famous carrot cake, and spends the dinner time telling her children fun and heartwarming stories about their grandmother.

One client who left her family's faith shortly after graduating from college, causing a lot of family friction, now celebrates her parents' wedding anniversary by going to temple on their special day. A friend of mine sends flowers on the first anniversary of the death of all her friend's parents and remembers them in her prayers. She sends a text to each friend on the death anniversary, saying something like: "Thinking of you and your mom on this day." These small traditions of thoughtfulness help build a bridge to the other side, increasing connection with our loved ones in the dream state and helping them to continue their spiritual progress on the other side.

Because these energy cords remain intact, our loved ones in heaven can still see us and visit us from time to time. When we tell their stories, when we think of them with love and joy, it sends them a burst of happy energy on the other side. Even small acts of kindness can greatly assist our loved ones in heaven. The father of one friend suffered from glaucoma toward the end of his life. Each year on the anniversary of his dad's passing, he makes a donation to the Glaucoma Research Foundation.

A client sent me this email last week:

Today is the anniversary of my brother's passing. I've pledged to do ten random acts of kindness on his anniversary each year. This year, I'm sending ten emails to people who have helped inspire me as a way of honoring my brother. So thank you for your podcast; your words of comfort about the afterlife have lifted me up and helped me process my grief.

## PENNIES FROM HEAVEN

My mother-in-law once asked me about the old expression "pennies from heaven." I explained to her that, since metal is a conductor of energy, it's easy for our loved ones to manipulate pennies, and many spirits use them as a way to communicate and connect with us. She smiled and said: "Oh, well that's not for me. When I die, I'll leave you quarters. What the heck are you going to do with a penny?" We laughed and agreed that, if I found a quarter in a weird place, I would know it was a hello from her.

Over the years, I have found quarters in the strangest places. I never carry cash, let alone change. Yet the day we returned home from my mother-in-law's funeral, we found a pile of quarters on the garage floor. When I was dealing with my breast cancer diagnosis, I found quarters at every doctor's visit.

I remember when I had to get my first mammogram after my cancer surgery. I was terrified. I sat in the parking lot for a long moment to steady my nerves. As soon as I stepped out of the car, I spotted a shiny new quarter on the ground and sighed with relief. I knew all would be well. Now I buy angel coins online and leave one in the parking lot each year when I get my mammogram, hoping that it brings someone else a bit of comfort. When I visit my dad at his nursing home, I often leave an angel coin for someone else to find. I drop one every time I visit a hospital or cemetery too.

These small, seemingly insignificant acts of kindness can be life-changing for the recipient. And when we perform these random acts of kindness in memory of a loved one in heaven, it reinforces our bond, our energy connection, with them. This helps to give them love and assists us in our grieving.

### Exercise: Meditation to Connect with a Loved One

This meditation will help you strengthen the bond with your loved ones and learn to reach out to them on the other side for help, to offer assistance, or just to connect with them once more.

Sit in a comfortable position and close your eyes. Imagine tree roots growing out of the soles of your feet and digging through the earth. Feel the center of your body rooted to the ground. Breathe deeply. Take several deep breaths as you imagine white light surrounding your entire body, enveloping you in its protective energy.

Imagine that you're walking through a lovely meadow. In front of you is the most glorious rainbow. Reach out and touch it. Notice how incredibly large it is. It extends higher than you can see and farther than you can take in. Now, take a deep breath and begin to walk through the rainbow. First, you walk through the red color. Breathe this color in and feel the fire of life and creation coursing through you, filling you with energy. Allow the vibrant red energy to flood through you. See it burning away old residues of insecurity, financial worries, and anxieties.

As you walk toward the orange ray—the color of a blazing sunset—you feel filled with creativity and passion. Your body, mind, and soul are one. Breathe in this orange light and see it filling up holes in your aura where you've felt unattractive, blocked, and stagnant. Allow the warm orange energy to heal your body, mind, and soul.

When you're ready, move forward into the yellow light. Breathe in the joyful, courageous, and powerful energy of this yellow light. Your own personal sun radiates out from your center. You feel grounded, centered, connected. The energy from the earth, the sun, and the rainbow fills you with love, light, and life force.

As you walk into the emerald light, your body is filled with love. Visualize the green light flooding into your heart center, scrubbing clean old residues of heartache and betrayal. Allow a force of love to awaken and grow inside of you.

Take a deep, cleansing breath and walk toward the sky-blue ray of the rainbow. You're reminded of the vastness of the sky and the ocean. You feel an infinite sense of peace and tranquility as the color soars through your body, purifying your thoughts and words.

As you walk into the indigo light, your third eye awakens and you release fully into the colors of the rainbow, allowing yourself to trust and see truth for the first time.

Finally, you move into the purple light—a perfect blend of the earth and sky—and you feel the union of the cosmos filling your body. You feel at one with the world, with your soul and your higher self. The gate to enlightenment is now opened for you.

As you walk out of the rainbow to the other side, you see in front of you a beautiful crystal cave. Walk inside and take a seat in the center of the cave. You feel calm, relaxed, and open. Look around the cave as you settle in. Feel the energy of the crystal walls pulsating and helping to lift your vibrations. You notice a crystal bridge leading from the cave to the other side. Ask your loved one to come across this bridge and greet you. Be patient and let yourself feel the sense of connection and love filling up the cave. See your loved one walking across the bridge and sitting across from you.

Take a moment to blend your energies. Use this time to discuss everything you've wanted to talk about. Ask how your loved one is doing and if there is a message for you. Ask if he or she needs anything from you. If you have a hard time visualizing a loved one, ask to see a special memory that you share.

When you've finished your conversation, see your loved one handing you a blue box. As you receive this gift, your loved one tells you that inside this box is a symbol of the sign you'll receive this week to validate this meditation experience. Open the box and peer inside. You may see a feather, a butterfly, a bird, or something completely unexpected. Thank your loved one and take a deep breath, knowing you can come back here anytime you need to for connection and love.

Take another deep breath and allow yourself a moment to sit in this energy of perfect peace and wholeness. When you're ready, reinforce the light around you and gently flutter your eyes open.

# Chapter 5

# THINGS THAT
# GO BUMP IN
# THE NIGHT

*Do not forget that we walk unwittingly among a
multitude of ghosts; they are invisible to everyone but
the messenger of souls.*

Arnaud Gelis

When I first realized I had intuitive abilities and started
taking classes to learn how to strengthen these gifts, I was
bothered by the wholly positive belief many teachers had
regarding the other side. Most of them claimed that there
was nothing negative to worry about there. One teacher
even taught us that we didn't need to practice psychic protection, because it indicated that our egoic, fearful mind
was in control.

Maybe so, but I believe we exist in a dualistic world.
There is up and down, left and right, night and day. As Sir
Francis Bacon wrote: "In order for the light to shine so
brightly, the darkness must be present." If you want to be a

practiced soul traveler, you have to study the darker, more negative aspects of the other side just as diligently as you focus on learning about the light.

While I was rushing off to classes on healing, chakras, Reiki, meditation, mediumship, and crystals, I was also experiencing fascinating soul-travel dreams in which I was a student in a type of astral psychic school. These began when I was pregnant with my youngest child and lasted for several years after she was born. These dreams often contained the same two people—a pregnant woman who knew she was having a boy, and a young man. The three of us stood in a line outside a classroom while a man or woman with a clipboard checked off our names as we entered. In the classroom, the three of us sat together, along with at least fifteen other students. We had a different teacher each night who presented a new lesson.

I didn't have these dreams every single night—more like once or twice a month. But I remember them as vividly as I can recall actual events that occurred in my waking life. One night, we were being taught how to fight negative energies. We were standing in a large hallway facing a stairwell when this "thing"—this mass of dark energy—formed into a hideous monster and approached us. Our teacher yelled at us to remember our light. I reached for my heart chakra, pulled light out of myself, and threw it at the dark mass. We all did. As our balls of light hit the dark entity, it didn't shrink or disappear. It transformed. Slowly but surely, it transformed into light.

This taught me that all beings have a dual nature. We all have darkness and light within us. The goal of any lightworker isn't to fight the darkness—either inside or outside of ourselves—but rather to transform it. Light exists in everyone and everything.

## NIGHTMARES

We can and often do encounter frightening things in our dreams. Nightmares, however, are most common in children. Around 25 percent of children from ages five through twelve report having frequent nightmares. And about half of all adults have occasional nightmares as well. Research leads many to believe that those who are fearful in waking life or who don't have strong boundaries tend to have more nightmares. People who've suffered a recent trauma or who are dealing with PTSD tend to have more frightening dreams.

Usually, nightmares occur to wake us up to issues we're not dealing with in our daily lives. A friend of mine whose company underwent a series of layoffs suddenly found herself doing the work of three people. She started having a recurring nightmare that she was being chased by a masked intruder wielding a knife. I advised her to fall asleep each night repeating to herself: "I will unmask my intruder tonight." After trying this for several nights, she was finally able to pull the mask off her frightening pursuer. The person she saw before her was her boss. She had been ignoring how much stress and anxiety her work was causing her. After this nightmare revelation, she spoke to her boss and they agreed that she could hire a part-time assistant. After this, the nightmares stopped.

While most nightmares are simply our brain's way of organizing and releasing our daily fears, some of these terrifying encounters are actually interactions with ghosts, astral shells (negative residue left by spirits), incubi or sucubi (demons), elementals, and shadow people. Many believe these negative entities that appear in our nightmares are fed by a form of energy vampirism. In other words, they feed off our fear.

Astral shells or astral vampires are believed by some to be the discarded, lowest energy of deceased people. It's as if, when we die, the best of us ascends to heaven while the lowest, basest, darkest aspects are discarded and remain partly alive by feeding off the energy of others when they're dreaming or visiting the astral planes in their sleep.

Incubi and succubi are demons who masquerade as beautiful sexual beings. They often appear in people's dreams to simulate a sexual experience. People report that, at the height of the dream's enjoyment, the being reveals itself for the demon it is and then feeds off a combination of sexual energy and fear.

Shadow people can be seen during both waking and sleeping hours. No one really knows what these beings are, but some believe they are visitors from other planets come to study us while we sleep. Some think they're another type of demonic entity, while others believe they are nothing more than the stressful residue our aura emits at the end of a difficult day. In nightmares, people report being stalked by these shadowy beings, who seem to feed off the fear we emit as they chase us in our dreams.

Some report seeing a being called Hat Man or Grinning Man in their nightmares, while others report seeing menacing shadowy figures staring at them from their bedroom doorways. In most of these encounters, the shadowy figures don't do anything but stare at the person, but these nightmares are often accompanied by profound sensations of fear and dread. Some researchers report that, after dreams of shadow people, negative events occur in the dreamer's life.

## HYPNAGOGIA–THE DOORWAY TO PSI

As we move from the awake state to the dreaming state, we enter a liminal space that occurs either as we're falling asleep (a hypnagogic state) or just before we're fully awake (a hypnopompic state). These liminal states of being are considered to be portals or doorways to psychic experiences.

Hypnagogia occurs as our brain-wave patterns transition from Beta (daily functioning) to Alpha (awake and alert, but restful), then into Theta (REM sleeping) and finally into Delta (deep sleep). When brain-wave patterns are recorded on an EEG, the wave patterns of these different brain states can be discerned. In a hypnagogic state, you may see flashes of color, orbs of light, or random faces. Some believe that this is the result of your brain organizing images in preparation for your dream time. You may hear random strains of music that you don't recognize, or you may hear your name being called.

Philosopher and esoteric writer Rudolf Steiner claims that this time between sleeping and waking holds the potential for powerful psychic experiences:

> Besides waking life and sleeping life there is a third state, even more important for intercourse with the spiritual world. I mean the state connected with the act of waking and the act of going to sleep, which lasts only for a few brief seconds. At the moment of going to sleep the spiritual world approaches us with power, but we immediately fall asleep, losing consciousness of what has passed through the soul.

As recounted in previous chapters, many have experienced visits from loved ones in heaven while in this liminal state between sleep and waking. Some have received incredible insights or clarity on a problem. But others have experienced really strange and negative things during this time as well.

In producer Lex Nover's fascinating book *Nightmareland*, he recounts two terrifying cases of nightmares that occurred during this liminal state of being. A Catholic monk told parapsychologist Charles Tart that, when he was still in that half-asleep/half-awake state one morning, he felt cold chills before hearing someone mumbling in the corner of his bedroom. When he looked over, he saw a small man who resembled a ventriloquist's doll speaking in a language he didn't understand. He got out of bed and grabbed the little man by the leg and threw him up to the ceiling.

The strange little man landed on the floor and scurried under the bed, then popped up on the other side of the bed and turned his head—just his head—as if he were talking to someone. "I heard him clear as a bell," the monk reported, "and had no trouble understanding. He said: 'We have him. Christ is burning. The Hummingbird Men have him.'" When the monk tried to grab him again, the odd little man simply disappeared. Prior to this, this monk claimed to be a rational man who didn't believe in the devil. After this experience, he wondered "if the fellow that we thought we had ridiculed into oblivion may actually exist."

Another strange case was reported to the Society for Psychical Research in 1917. Walter Franklin Prince dreamed that a woman asked him to witness her death. In this dream, the young woman asked him to hold her hand throughout the experience. He reports feeling her grip his hand and then being horrified to realize in the next moment that he was holding a severed head. When members of the Society looked into Prince's story, they discovered that, on the same day that he had this dream, a young woman in Long Island, where Prince lived, had knelt in front of an oncoming train and been decapitated. The incident took place just six miles from the doctor's home. It is possible that Prince was open to connecting with the spirit of this distraught woman in the dream state because they were geographically close and his soul heard her calls for help.

# SLEEP PARALYSIS

Sleep paralysis occurs when we come partially awake during the REM cycle. During an episode of sleep paralysis, people report feeling a presence in the room. They are unable to move any part of their body except their eyes. Sleep paralysis is usually accompanied by overwhelming feelings of fear and dread, and reports of terrifying entities that exist on astral planes that can only interact with us during the dream state.

In *Dark Intrusions*, Louis Proud, a writer and researcher specializing in anomalous phenomena, describes his sleep paralysis experiences as life-and-death battles.

> During the sleep paralysis state, I feel that my attacker is trying to draw me into an extremely deep, permanent sleep, and if I let myself succumb, I will not be able to wake up. Imagine you're underwater, with lead weights attached to your feet, and you're trying to swim to the surface, but the weight keeps dragging you down. That's what it feels like. The reason I manage to break through the surface, so to speak, and have on every occasion, is because of my powerful will to survive—which is something we all possess.

Of course, we are always partially paralyzed during sleep to prevent us from acting out our dreams. And many believe that the sense of fear or dread experienced in sleep paralysis is really just an instinctive reaction to being aware of our temporary state of paralysis. However, as Proud points out:

Assuming that the astral body leaves the physical body every time we sleep, it would not be unreasonable to state the only difference between a Sleep Paralysis sufferer and a non-Sleep Paralysis sufferer is that the former has some awareness of these astral experiences and is able to remember them in the morning.

During sleep paralysis, people have often reported seeing a hideous being sitting atop them. People who've experienced this wake up to discover that they can't move. Many report seeing a monstrous, frightening old woman sitting on them trying to steal their energy. Some believe these astral beings feed off the fear we release when we see them in our dreams.

Sleep paralysis has been reported throughout history and across many cultures. In Japan, they call it *kanashibari*, which means "bound by metal." In Germany, they talk about the *alp*, a demonic elf who paralyzes people in their sleep and attacks them. In Brazil, legends abound about the *pisadeira*, a demonic roof-dwelling woman with long nails who preys on people's energy while they sleep. The Inuits tell of a shapeless, faceless presence that tries to possess souls during sleep. Hawaiian lore warns of "night marchers," vengeful dead warriors whose presence is accompanied by drumbeats and heavy footsteps.

In *The Terror That Comes in the Night*, David Hufford, professor of humanistic medicine at the University of Pennsylvania, writes about an elderly fisherman in Newfoundland who told him about an experience he had while living in a bunkhouse in Labrador as a young man. One of his fellow fishermen met a woman and tried to seduce her. When she rebuffed his advances, he warned her that he would appear that night in her dreams as a nightmarish hag. That night, the fisherman told Hufford, he watched as this awful man removed his clothes, knelt by his bed, and recited the Lord's Prayer backward. He then took out his knife and began attacking his bedside table.

The next morning, the young woman said she'd seen the man standing over her in the middle of the night with a knife in his hand. Had this woman seen the astral form of her assailant because he'd planted the idea in her mind when he threatened her? Or had he actually managed to project his soul into her bedroom?

Our emotions greatly affect our dreams, and this is no different when we're dealing with sleep paralysis. Proud claims that, when he feels nervous, stressed, or depressed, his sleep paralysis experiences become more frequent and more intense. This makes me wonder whether some of the scary experiences people report are really aspects of their psyches crying out for attention and release. Dion Fortune wrote in *Psychic Self-Defense* that we can be haunted by our own thoughts and emotions because "[what] we extrude from our auras will return to us in due course. Any strong emotion is a source of astral energy, and fear and pain are no exceptions." However, she also mentions that there are very real and negative entities existing on the astral plane who feed off our negative energies.

Astral traveler Jurgen Ziewe describes an experience he had while visiting the lower levels of the astral plane. He saw a man being eaten alive by millions of maggots. The thought appeared in his mind that these maggots symbolized how the man, in his actual life, was "eating himself alive" with negative thoughts and lack of self-love. This suggests that some of the frightening nightmarish experiences we have while sleeping are connected to our own inner fears and that our souls are simply manifesting these experiences to make us face our deepest fears about ourselves.

One client shared with me that, after going through a spiritual awakening, she joined a church and began praying each night before bed. One night, she fell asleep reciting the Twenty-third Psalm and awoke hours later to see a scary old woman sitting on her chest. She couldn't move or speak. Then she remembered the prayer she'd been reciting as she fell alseep and forced herself to say the only words she could remember: "The Lord is my shepherd." The old hag vanished, but the woman was left shaken and unable to fall back asleep.

When the woman visited her pastor the next day to seek his advice, he told her that he'd heard the same story many times. These negative entities were nothing more than astral bullies, he said. Give them attention—your fear—and they will stay. But if you choose to stay strong in your light, joy, and faith, they will get bored and find a new victim to bully. "When a person chooses the light over the dark, there are forces who will try to scare them away from their spiritual progress. Keep strong," he advised her, "and these attacks will stop."

Science disagrees with this spiritual view, however, and believes that sleep paralysis is nothing more than your brain waking up before your body. I believe that science and spirituality can find some common ground here. It could be that the fear and chest pressure felt during sleep paralysis are really just our astral selves returning to the physical body via the silver cord located in the chest.

A phenomenon called "hypnagogic jerks" occur when the body startles as we're falling asleep or waking up. Some sleep researchers believe this is the result of our waking, egoic mind fighting for control as it's asked to surrender to sleep and allow the unconscious mind to take over. While this may be true in many cases, it could also be the feeling of our soul returning to its physical body. Dion Fortune warned that occultists often wait until their victims are asleep to attack them psychically, because sleep is the one time when our defenses are down. Fortunately, there are several ways we can protect ourselves from these psychic attacks. Whether they originate from an aspect of our hidden fears, are the result of our physical bodies resisting sleep or waking up, or are indeed evidence of negative entities, when we practice psychic protection, we can fend off these frightening experiences.


## PSYCHIC ATTACKS

Psychic attacks occur when any negative energy is directed at you—either from others or from within yourself. These attacks come in many forms:

- Gossip or rumors
- Back-stabbing actions

- Malicious or vengeful thoughts

- Being open to negative people while in a compromised state (i.e., partaking in alcohol or recreational drugs)

- Rebounding negative energy you sent out to others

- Self-sabotaging behaviors and thoughts

- Physically working on negative people (i.e., therapists or healers working on clients who have a lot of negative energy)

- Doing intuitive or energy work without grounding your energy

- Working or living in a toxic environment

In addition to these more external causes, however, your own state of mind can leave you open to psychic attack as well.

When you're experiencing an excessive amount of guilt, low self-esteem, depression, worry, or anxiety, you leave yourself open to psychic attack from a variety of sources. If you're highly sensitive and intuitive, you're more susceptible to psychic attack and must be extra vigilant about keeping your protection shield around you. The best defense against this is a strong, healthy aura. Unfortunately, however, we can be strong and protected during our waking hours and still be open to negative energy during our dreaming time.

In *Psychic Self-Defense*, Dion Fortune tells of a psychic attack she experienced in her sleep while staying at an occult school in England. One of the residents, whom Fortune refers to as "Miss L," was angry at Fortune for rebuffing her affections.

> That night I was afflicted with the most violent
> nightmare I have ever had in my life, waking
> from sleep with the terrible sense of oppression
> on my chest as if someone was holding me down.
> I saw distinctly the head of Miss L reduced to the
> size of an orange floating in the air at the foot of
> my bed and snapping its teeth at me. It was the
> most malignant thing I have ever seen.

Was Miss L causing this nightmare with some type of astral projection? Or was this scary vision the result of manifested thought? Indeed, it is possible that our thoughts are so powerful that they can even impact someone else's dreams.

In *Nightmareland*, Lex Nover writes about a man named Harry who was attacked by his deceased wife in his sleep. The nightmarish situation began seventeen years after his wife had died. He dreamed that she appeared to him in flowing white robes and had glowing red eyes. When she tried to kiss him, Harry woke up. The ghostly image began appearing several times a week in Harry's nightmares, each dream becoming more intense and leaving him depressed, losing weight, and questioning his own sanity.

One night when he slept as a guest at his sister's home, she went to check on him in the night. She found him lying quite frozen on the bed with his mouth hanging open. When she approached him to check if he was still breathing, she reported walking into a spot that was so cold it temporarily froze her in place. She pushed through the frigid sensation and reached for her brother. Then she felt an invisible presence between them. "In that second, something invisible writhed and twisted between us. Whatever it was, I could feel it physically. And then inches from my eyes, a misty gray, vaporous mass spiraled ceilingward." Both Harry and his sister reported an eerie laughter echoing throughout the room.

Harry checked himself into a hospital for psychiatric testing, but was deemed healthy and well. Doctors gave him medication for his anxiety and sent him home. Just a few days later, Harry died of a heart attack. Was his deceased wife so angry that she psychically attacked him from beyond the grave? Or was another negative entity masquerading as his wife to attack him for some unknown reason?

It's also possible for our own thoughts and emotions to attack someone else unknowingly in the dream state. Occultist Michelle Belanger, author of *Psychic Dreamwalking: Explorations at the Edge of Self*, believes that she's been the unwitting perpetrator of a psychic dream attack. One evening when she was feeling depleted of energy, she dreamed that she was a vampire biting her neighbor's neck. The next day, she awoke feeling invigorated and energized. When her haggard-looking neighbor came over to talk to her, he had a hickey-shaped mark on his neck and told her he'd had the strangest dream the night before that Michelle had bitten him.

If we're all connected by a collective universal consciousness, then it makes sense that we can visit one another in the dream space—for good or nefarious reasons. There-fore, it's imperative that we learn to practice good psychic protection when we're awake *and* when we're asleep.

## PSYCHIC PROTECTION

Each of us is surrounded by a field of our own unique, personal energy called the aura. For most of us, this aura extends about seven feet around us and acts like a gate or a filter. It decides what energy gets in and what energy stays out. However, there are several things that can weaken or damage the aura—for instance, health issues, depression, anger, or sadness. Learning to practice good psychic pro-tection techniques can help you maintain a healthy, strong aura. If you make it a habit to ground your energy every day, putting up your psychic shield and clearing your energy each evening, your energy will be your own and your aura will be sparkly clean. Moreover, you'll be pro-tected while dreaming.

Think of your aura as the home you live in. We all work hard to keep our homes protected. We have windows and doors that lock. Some of us have alarm systems or door-bells with wireless cameras and other methods of keeping our homes secure. And you must have a similar system in place to protect your aura from unwanted energy.

Let's start by looking at your chakras. You have seven main chakras that are centered along your spine. Each chakra stores a different type of energy that is projected into your aura. The root chakra, for example, located at the base of your spine, stores energy connected to your feelings of safety and security, while your heart chakra holds energy related to relationships and love. As you move through your day, you're bombarded by situations that effect your energy.

If you're empathic, your chakras will open easily to connect with others. If you start your day by grabbing a cup of coffee and you find yourself standing in line behind someone who's having a really rough time, your heart chakra may pop open without your conscious awareness. As your heart sends the individual love and light, you may inadvertently link in with that person's emotions and pick up their stress.

Every day, your chakras are bombarded with positive and negative energy coming at you. This is why good psychic protection techniques are so crucial to your vitality and life-force energy. At work, you may encounter an angry customer who makes your solar plexus chakra, the seat of will and confidence, shrink in fear. When you get home, you find an unexpected bill in the mail that you aren't sure you can pay. These fears get stored in your root chakra. Now you're feeling sad and anxious, but then you see that your partner has made a lovely dinner for you and you get an email from your boss thanking you for doing a great job with that angry customer and your heart chakra fills with strong energies of love and contentment.

In the jungle, predators look for weak, distracted, or injured prey. Similarly, criminals look for victims who are distracted. When psychologists ask criminals how they pick their victims, they tend to say things like: "She wasn't paying attention." Or "He was all alone. It was easy." In the world of energy, negativity can cling to us when we are similarly distracted. To avoid being an easy target for negative energy, you must be strong within and ask for protection from your guides and angels, so that you aren't vulnerable to negativity.

In the morning, when you're in the shower or waiting for your coffee, simply close your eyes for a few moments and imagine a grounding technique that works for you. You can visualize tree roots extending from the soles of your feet going down through the floor below you and then down into the earth. You can picture an anchor coming out of your root chakra and going into the earth, rooting itself deep inside the Earth's core. Or you can imagine light shining down on you, pouring into your crown chakra at the top of your head, then flowing down through your body, coming out of your feet and extending down into the earth. See two tunnels of white light extending from your feet going down into the ground below you and wrapping around roots deep down in the earth. Once you've firmly visualized one of these grounding techniques, imagine your psychic shield (see below).

When you get home, take your shoes off at the door to symbolize leaving the day behind you. Try to do something grounding—take a walk around your neighborhood, go outside and water your garden, or just walk around in your bare feet. Do something creative or meditative to relax and restore your energy. If something upsetting occurred with someone during your day, place all ten of your fingertips together and say: "I break up and dispel any and all energy between this person (say their full name) and me" and then pull your hands apart and shake off the energy.

Take a salt bath if you feel that you're carrying some-one else's energy around with you. Add a cup of Epsom salts and a half cup of sea salt to a running bath and soak for twenty minutes. If you've been bombarded by negative dream experiences, you can place four protective crystals under the four corners of your bed. Any black or brown stone works great—hematite, black tourmaline, onyx, jet, or jasper. Say a prayer to your higher power before falling asleep asking for protection, like this one I was taught as a child:

Bless this bed that I lie on
Four corners to my bed
Four angels around my head
One to watch and one to pray
And two to guide me on my way.

Then visualize and reaffirm your psychic shield of protection around you as you sleep.

We all need to shield ourselves before we go out the door *and* before we fall asleep. Just as you put on clothes to protect your body, you must put on your psychic shield to protect your energy. Be sure to create your psychic protection shield both in the morning and in the evening.

To create a basic shield of protection, sit in a comfortable, quiet place with your eyes closed and ground your energy. Imagine tree roots coming out of the soles of your feet, pushing through the floor below you, and extending deep into the soil. Visualize a bright, powerful, protective light shining down from the heavens onto your body and say to yourself: "This shield protects me from negative thoughts, people, experiences, memories, entities, and actions."

Next, imagine a dog running toward you and see the dog bouncing off the light of your shield. Then picture a charging bull running toward you and see the bull also being pushed away by the strength of your shield. Finally, imagine a group of arrows coming toward you from all directions and see these bouncing off your shield as well. Together, these images will activate and reinforce the strength of your shield.

Keep in mind that creating a shield of protection around you is not enough. To activate the shield, you have to visualize something trying to penetrate it and being forced away. Your psychic shield will remain energized for about ten to twelve hours. You can replenish your shield with more light throughout the day. And be sure to repeat these steps in the evening to protect you in your dream time.

## CORD-CUTTING

Cords are energetic attachments that form between people and aspects of ourselves. We share both positive and negative energy through these cords, and the deeper the connection, the stronger the cord. You can be corded to your spouse, your partner, your children, your parents, your siblings, and your friends. But you can also have cords with neighbors, co-workers, acquaintances, and old loves.

Narcissists or negative people can use these cords subconsciously to drain your energy. If they think negative thoughts about you, you will feel this through the cord. How do you know if you are connected to someone with a negative cord? When the exchange of energy is imbalanced, your cord becomes muddy and your energy can get blocked. If someone is obsessing over you and not letting you go, this can also deplete your energy. You may think of them and wonder why you can't stop remembering these painful times. They can also appear in your dreams.

When one of my clients was divorcing a narcissist, he had recurring nightmares that his ex was trying to break into his home. These dreams were detailed and specific. In one, he saw that his partner was removing the locks with a quiet drill in order to sneak in unnoticed. In another, he saw him quietly cutting the wires outside his home so he couldn't call for help. Over and over, the theme of "quiet intrusion" repeated in his dreams, leading him to believe that his former partner was corded to his energy. Once he started to practice cord-cutting and visualizing his psychic protection, the dreams stopped and his energy levels soared.

These are some signs that you might be negatively corded to someone:

- You may feel strong emotions toward the person to whom you're corded. In healthy relationships, these emotions are joyful and loving. In toxic relationships, these emotions are anger, fear, anxiety, and sadness.

- People may pop into your mind frequently. You may dream of them or bump into them in town. They will call you soon after you think of them. This can happen with positive cording as well.

- You may get a headache or stomach ache when you're around an individual.

- You may feel tired after being around someone.

- You may have a hard time letting go of the past with someone and not be able to move on. If a relationship didn't end properly or left feelings of regret, anger, and sadness, you may have a negative cord.

- If you're not able to let go of someone, or if someone just can't seem to let go of you even though you know the relationship has ended, you may have a negative cord with this person.

We can also be corded to aspects of ourselves that are negative—for instance, in cases of addictive behaviors, energy blocks, or repeating patterns of behavior that are holding you back. If you've walked away from a bad habit or way of thinking, you can still have a cord to a part of you that craves this bad habit or continues to think negatively. It's important to cut these cords as well.

A common nightmare many experience is being chased by an unknown "someone," only to turn around and discover that the person doing the terrifying chasing is actually themselves. This is often a sign that you have a negative cord to an aspect of yourself that needs to be healed. Cords can also be created between ourselves and memories. If you feel triggered by a painful memory, or if you feel that someone is trying to send you negative energy and it's impacting your dreams, consider doing a cord-cutting meditation to sever the emotional pain connected to the person or memory (see below).

There are many ways to cut negative cords. One simple process involves guided imagery. Just sit or lie down in a quiet place where you'll be undisturbed and imagine yourself and the person to whom you're corded standing facing each other—in a garden, on a stage, or by the ocean. Take some time to allow yourself to visualize this fully. Mentally scan your energy and ask to see the cords that connect you. These may appear as ropes, chains, threads, sewer pipes, hoses, hooks, wires, or plugs. The length, color, shape, size, and texture will be different for each cord.

Cords can hook into your energy anywhere on your body—your head, your ankles, your shoulders—but most cords tend to be concentrated along your torso, especially on your back, near your heart, or in your stomach. Cords usually line up with your chakras. If someone is trying to take your power at work, for example, there may be a cord attached to your solar plexus chakra. If a partner has broken your heart, there may be one at your heart chakra.

If you have a hard time with visualization, ask your angel to come and help you. Many call on the Archangel Michael to come with his mighty sword and help cut these cords. You can also call on your spirit guide, your guardian angel, or a loved one in heaven for help. Try holding black kyanite during the process to protect your energy and sever unwanted ties. After the cord is cut, journal any emotions or memories that come to the surface. Then take the black kyanite and sweep it around your aura to reinforce that any and all negative energy is now dissipated.

After you cut a cord, distance yourself from the person as much as possible. Stay off social media; don't return calls or texts. When you cut a cord to someone, they will feel it without knowing why. You may hear from them and they will often try to placate you. Sometimes they will even try to make you angry or afraid. But any reaction you allow will just re-establish the connection, so do your best to ignore these attempts. Moreover, you must repeat this process until the toxic person, memory, or emotion is completely gone. Luckily, cord-cutting is easy once you get the hang of it. When you can observe and recognize the abuse without experiencing the sadness, you know you are free.

If you want to cut a cord to a negative aspect of yourself, follow the same steps, but visualize yourself corded to a symbol, memory, or image of yourself engaging in this negative pattern and cut the cord. You can also cut cords to a deceased person. If you had issues with a relative who has passed and this relationship is still wreaking havoc in your life through guilt, anger, shame, or regret, you can do a cord-cutting meditation.

Here's another technique you can try. Write your name on one piece of paper, then write the name of the person to whom you're corded on another piece of paper. Roll up each piece of paper and tie it with a string. Then tie both pieces of paper together. Cut the string while repeating the steps outlined above.

If you're cutting the cord between you and someone you see often—a family member, a boss, or a co-worker—there is a good chance you two will reconnect. That's why it's important to be vigilant with your energy. If negative emotions recur or you have another negative dream about the person, just repeat the cord-cutting technique you chose.

When you begin to practice these techniques on a regular basis—shielding your energy, protecting your space while you sleep, and cord-cutting—any negative dreams you've been experiencing will dissipate. It's so important to remember that we have control over our energy when we're awake *and* when we're asleep. As you learn to work with the powerful force of your own energy, you will realize that you can utilize the sleep state for interacting with your deceased loved ones, guides, and angels. And when you practice good psychic protection, you can enter your dream state with confidence and use this sacred time to receive guidance, insight, and profound healing.

**Exercise: Cord-Cutting Meditation**
When you're ready to do a cord-cutting meditation, make sure you have time to be alone. A good time to do this is right before bed or first thing in the morning. Light a candle, play some peaceful music, and call on your guides and angels. Crystals that are excellent to use for this meditation include black kyanite, selenite, or nuumite. Consider journaling about the relationship you are addressing. Write down all the positive and negative lessons, memories, and emotions connected to it. See if you can identify any patterns.

Close your eyes and do some deep breathing to bring yourself into a calm, relaxed state, then mentally scan your body and see where the cord is attached. Follow the cord and see where the other end of the cord is attached. If you have a hard time visualizing, simply pay attention to who pops into your thoughts.

Now notice the cord. What kind of cord is it? Does it look old or new? Is it tattered and frayed? Strong or weak? See yourself holding the cord and take a moment to send light through it to clear and cleanse it of negativity. Ask if the cord has a message for you. What purpose, what lesson, is this relationship teaching you? After you've been able to visualize the cord existing between you and the other person or circumstance, hold out your dominant hand and imagine a cord-cutting tool appearing there—a pair of scissors, shears, or a sword. Visualize yourself cutting the cord. Check to see if anything spills out of it. Visualize any residue in your energy from the cut cord dissolving and disappearing entirely.

Say something affirmative and definitive, like: "I cut this cord of negativity between us in all directions of time. The lessons remain, but the negativity is now severed forever." Dissolve any residue with the intention of your light. It's important at this stage of your meditation to visualize the stump of the cord (residue left over after cutting it) dissolving so it doesn't reattach and grow like a weed. I like to visualize myself holding a sword of light—a flaming sword to burn away all residue. Sometimes, especially if it's a strong or old cord, I ask Archangel Michael, the angel of protection, and Archangel Raphael, the angel of healing, to step in with their swords of light to help me.

Surround yourself with light. Once the cord has been cut and fully removed from your energy, see yourself surrounded in a thick layer of golden light to seal in your aura. Visualize the other person walking away until you can no longer see them.

# Chapter 6

# HEALING DREAMS

*Our dreams are free medicine.*

Lori Dechar

If dreams are powerful enough to connect us with departed loved ones or show us glimpses into the future, can they also help us to heal physically and emotionally? Research into the history of healing dreams shows us that they can. In "Galen, On the Diagnosis of Dreams," classisist Steven Oberhelman writes: "Divination through dreams was acknowledged by nearly every ancient physician from Hippocrates and Herophilus to the Empiricists, Rufus of Ephesus and Galen." In fact, Rufus believed that dreams were one of the most important diagnostic tools physicians had at their disposal. When Greek physician Galen was suffering from a subdiaphragmatic abscess, he had two dreams in which he saw himself opening an artery between his thumb and forefinger and letting it bleed. He tried this procedure in waking life and it cured him.

The ancient Greeks believed so much in the healing power of dreams that they practiced something called "dream incubation," in which the afflicted traveled to a dream temple and underwent a series of purification rites, including fasting, exercise, bathing, prayers, and offerings to the gods. Then a dream priest anointed them with oils said to induce dream recall and sent them to sleep in a section of the temple. In the morning, the patients discussed their dreams with the priests, who interpreted them to gain insight into the ailment and the cure.

When we set the intention to dream with a specific purpose, we can receive invaluable insights into emotional and physical ailments. My neighbor started having a series of health issues in the 1980s that doctors couldn't diagnose. Her bones hurt, she was constantly tired, and she had no energy. Yet test after test showed that there was nothing wrong with her. She decided to pray about this each night before falling asleep. After a few weeks of this prayer ritual, she awoke from a dream to find that she'd written a name on a pad of paper during the night. When she looked in the phone book, she found a doctor listed with that last name. She called the doctor's office, made an appointment, and finally received a correct diagnosis. She had Lyme disease and the doctor she had identified in her dream was the only doctor in her town at that time who knew how to diagnose it.

# PHYSICAL HEALING

Our souls are always trying to communicate and connect with us to share meaningful messages of healing, precognition, and inspiration. In his book *Love, Medicine and Miracles*, surgeon Bernie Siegal shares a dream a man had in which people were piercing his neck with long needles. He then dreamed that someone was placing hot coals under his chin. Believing the dreams were trying to tell him something, he went to see his doctor and was shocked to discover he was in the very early stages of thyroid cancer.

When a client of mine was six months pregnant, she began having recurring dreams that her child would be born early. She reported them to her doctor, who shrugged them off as the normal worries of a first-time mom. But my client knew something was wrong and insisted the doctor do more tests. They discovered a problem with her uterus that created a risk for premature labor. She was put on bed rest and she delivered her baby safely—at thirty-seven weeks.

Many soul travelers report giving healing energy in their dreams. Doctors, nurses, therapists, chiropractors, Reiki practitioners, and holistic healers have all reported helping people in the dream state. They describe dreams in which they are in a room with someone—usually someone they don't know—working energetically on the body to achieve a state of balance.

One nurse often has dreams that she is healing people with rainbow lights in a location on the beach. Her clients are on a massage table lulled by the sound of the ocean and calmed by the rainbow lights she directs to their chakras. A

Reiki Master I know has dreams that he is giving Reiki to someone in a healing temple. He describes a large building with several columns and stairs leading up to the healing room, where beautiful music plays while he directs healing energy to people surrounded by a team of helpers that includes angels.

I've had several dreams in which I'm invited to a church, temple, or healing circle and asked to pass on healing energy. These dreams began after I had my first Reiki attunement and they continue today. Sometimes I am just putting my hands on people's heads or shoulders during these dreams and channeling healing energy to them. At other times, I am working with a circle of healers surrounding a table and we are sending light energy to an individual as a group.

## EMOTIONAL HEALING

Healing dreams come in many forms. Some warn us of health issues while others bring messages of emotional healing. After one friend's divorce, she was unable to cry. It was as though her heart had hardened itself against feeling any pain. She walked through the divorce proceedings numbed to any emotion—positive or negative. Her grandmother began appearing in her dreams telling her to release her pain, but even this didn't help. Then one night, she dreamed that her grandmother was combing her hair while singing a lullaby, just as she had done for her as a little girl. The dream brought up so many old emotions that, upon waking, she was finally able to cry and begin the healing process.

I often have dreams in which I'm sitting at an oceanside café giving readings or just listening to people's stories. I never shared these dreams with anyone because they felt too personal, but then I started getting emails from people who listened to my podcast, *Psychic Teachers*. People I'd never met wrote to me about having dreams in which they were sitting with me at an oceanside café or walking along the ocean "near a restaurant" with me. One man wrote:

> Dear Samantha. I am not psychic, nor do I believe in all this mumbo jumbo. But my wife made me listen to all your podcasts while we were driving to Texas to see her family. I didn't even think I was listening. I'd just had a fight with my stepmom. My dad recently died and my stepmom is refusing to give us his Purple Heart or really anything of his. You talk so much on your podcast about forgiveness. There is no way I could ever forgive my stepmom.
>
> But that first night in Texas, I had a dream in which you and I were walking by the ocean. You said my dad was sad over his wife's actions and that he's working to help her see to giving me his Purple Heart. But he said to tell me that he isn't with his things. It's all just things. Even the Purple Heart. He's with me, his grandkids, he's in our hearts. He said he loved me and was so proud

of me. You even told me that he'd show me a sign to make sure I knew this wasn't a dream.

When I woke up, I said to my wife: "No more podcasts. This is flipping me out." But that night, I went out on the deck to get a break from my in-laws and smoke a cigarette. I couldn't get the dream out of my head. I was alone and I said to no one: "If that dream was real, where's my goddamn sign?" And you know what, Samantha? I saw a shooting star. Right then. The second after I said those words.

Another woman emailed:

I know we haven't met but listening to you each week, I feel like I know you, so maybe that's why I had this dream. We were sitting at a café and the ocean was behind you. I was asking you about my job, and you told me that I was going to get a promotion out of the blue but that this was really a test. You said I had a history of taking the safe route, but I was here to learn to take risks and that it was time for me to take this risk and start the business my husband and I have been planning for years.

That week I was offered a promotion! But I remembered the dream and said no to the promotion, the safe route. My husband and I were just approved for a loan and our new online business will go live next month. I feel like that dream allowed me to drop years of emotional fears that held me back. I know it sounds weird to thank you when it was probably just a dream—but thank you.

For years, I thought my dreams of counseling people at an oceanside café were just my unconscious brain's way of preparing me for giving readings in real life. But after receiving so many emails from listeners who "met" me at an oceanside café in their dreams, I have to wonder if I am indeed offering healing and readings on my soul journeys.

Dreams can offer us so much emotional healing. Before my father was diagnosed with Alzheimer's, I dreamed he went missing while canoeing. I prayed aloud: "Dear God, please send my dad home to us." Instantly, three priests appeared wearing brown robes with white rope belts. They carried balls of incense and seemed to be blessing the land and the water. I found them very comforting, but I couldn't make any sense of the dream. Today, my dad can't remember who I am. It *is* as if he's missing. I feel the dream was telling me that his guides (symbolized by the priests) were watching over him.

In the early stages of my father's illness, I started having dreams in which we sipped tea at my oceanside café and discussed religion, politics, and the deeper mysteries of life, just as we had in the old days. Nothing special happened in these dreams, but we connected and shared the way we used to. In one dream, we were talking about politics and the state of the world when I heard an alarm clock. "Whoops!" my dad said. "Looks like it's time to go." As I watched, it was almost as if a string attached to his back pulled him through the ocean scene and out of my dream. I awoke to find my alarm clock ringing, just as it had in the dream.

These dream visits continued until my father reached the later stages of Alzheimer's. Today, he can barely communicate other than to point or smile. Then one afternoon, he suddenly became very lucid. For the first time in almost a year, he made direct eye contact with me and asked: "Will you come back when you die?" I wasn't sure if he knew what he was saying because he often confused his words and gestures. "They keep telling me I can come back if I want to," he continued. When I asked him to tell me more, he said that every night when he falls asleep, a staircase appears in his room. "You're always there to help me up the stairs," he said. "And when I get to the top, you tell me it's okay to go 'over the bridge.'" But he was adamant that he was not ready for that journey.

I knew instantly that, in my soul travels, I was trying to help prepare my dad for his final transition. The knowledge stunned me and I now cherish this conversation as a great gift because it showed me that, at least at night in his soul travels, my father was still connecting with those he loved.

## LIFE REVIEW

Near-death experiencers have taught us that, when we die, we have to undergo a life review in which we watch all the highs and lows from our lives. We get to see all the good we did, but also all the opportunities for doing good that we missed. It can be a wonderful and difficult process all at the same time. After sharing my dad's story on my podcast, a listener wrote that, shortly before her mom died from Alzheimer's complications, she spoke about dreams in which she was seated in a movie theater watching scenes from her life. She kept telling her daughter: "I should have laughed more."

Healing dream experiences like this can also bring profound awareness to difficult relationships in our lives. I've always had a strained relationship with my mother. Then one night, I had a fascinating dream. I was sitting at the ocean-side café with my mother seated across from me. Her demeanor was relaxed and casual; her elbows were on the table and she was gazing at me lovingly.

"So how's it going?" she said. "I mean, really, how are you? When you asked me to do this lifetime with you and be a true bitch, I knew it would help your soul. But I've got to admit it has been hard for me. I hate being this mean all the time. It feels just awful."

When I reached for her hand, I felt her warmth flow through me. "I know, but it is really helping me. I understand what a sacrifice this is for you. But thank you. Truly. We'll get through this together, you and I. Besides, it's just this one lifetime and then you can go back to being you."

This dream rocked my world. Was my mother's soul actually kind and loving? Had she agreed to incarnate as a thorn in my heart to *help* me? And if so, why? Why would I choose this? And then it dawned on me that maybe I wouldn't be a kind, caring person if I'd had a kind, caring mom. Maybe I'd be a spoiled brat or a shallow soul. I probably wouldn't be psychic. Growing up with the constant need to tune in to my mother's ever-changing moods had finely tuned my own intuition and enabled me to do this work. It also helped me grow in empathy and compassion for all souls.

My therapist told me that this was just a dream—my subconscious way of reconciling a lack of mother love. Maybe. Maybe so. But could it be that we really *do* choose our parents—even the ones who really shouldn't be parents? Maybe our souls look at these lifetimes as marathon races, not sprints—as a way for us to learn and grow and develop. Having a difficult mom definitely taught me how to be a good mom myself. And that, to me, is all that really matters in life. My children know they are loved unconditionally. They understand that they will always come first in my life. My two sisters are also wonderful mothers who cherish their children.

A year after this dream experience with my mother, I dreamed that I was riding in the car with her and my sisters. She was driving erratically, speeding and weaving in and out of traffic. I yelled at her to pull over and told her to get in the back seat and put her seat belt on. As I was walking around to the driver's side of the car, I saw three elderly women approaching—the same three women who showed up in my sister's dream on the eve of her wedding, the same three women who warned me that my daughter would be born a week early. I smiled warmly at them and waved. The oldest one grabbed my hand, pulled me into a hug, and said: "Your breaking a generational chain." "Good for you!" the youngest woman added. Then the third woman poked her head in the car window and said to my sisters: "You ladies are doing a great job!"

These dream experiences have taught me that we choose our parents for a variety of reasons, but mainly to help grow our souls. Soon after this dream, I had another in which my sisters and I were standing in a circle in a beautiful, lush forest with my niece, the eldest grandchild. My oldest sister was holding an ornately wrapped gift box. She passed it to my other sister, who then passed it on to me. I smiled happily in the dream and passed the box on to my niece. Then we all surrounded her in a warm hug. Three months later, my niece told the family that she and her husband were expecting their first child—a baby girl. The generational chain has indeed been broken.

## TRANSFORMATIONAL HEALING

When our souls travel during the dream time, we can send and receive healing. But we can also transform our energy by awakening to new methods of interacting with our waking world. This is often a crossover experience connected to the work we're doing throughout the day.

A student in one of my intuitive development classes told me how he'd been trying to forgive his dad for abandoning him. He was working with a therapist who guided him to do some inner-child work. One night, he dreamed that he and his dad were fishing. His dad explained that he'd wanted to be there for him, but had been incarcerated for drugs shortly after he was born. Apparently the student's mother had gotten a divorce and asked her ex-husband never to contact them again.

In the dream, the father felt a tug on his fishing pole and said: "Looks like I got something!" When he pulled the pole out of the water, there was a baseball attached to the end of the fishing line. He handed it to his son and said: "For you, son."

When the student awoke, he wrote everything down and called his mother. Finally, the whole story came out. "But why would he give me a baseball in the dream?" he asked. His mother sighed and said: "Your dad and I met at college. He was there on a baseball scholarship until he had a pretty bad car accident that left him unable to pitch. He lost his scholarship and that's when his troubles with drugs began." This transformative dream allowed my student to finally forgive his father. "I no longer saw him as a deadbeat who left his family," he said. "Now I see that he was just a damaged soul broken down by life's challenges."

Another student from the same class shared a series of transformative dreams with me. One day after work, she was mugged on the street walking to her car. The experience left her paralyzed with fear and angry at God and her angels. Where were they when this happened? One night, she had a dream that she was walking through a crowded mall where everyone was wearing earmuffs.

Each person was walking with a beautiful angel by their side. I watched as the angels whispered information to their person, but they couldn't hear their angel because of the earmuffs. Most of them were staring at their phones too. It was such a silly yet profound dream that I couldn't get it out of my head for days.

I went back to my journals. I try to write down my dreams, thoughts, and worries as much I can. When I flipped to the weeks leading up to the mugging, I was shocked by what I had written. Three days before the mugging, I wrote in my journal that I kept hearing the song "Please Don't Go" in my head. Two nights before it, I dreamed that my boss asked me to work from home that week. And then the night before the mugging, I dreamed that I was walking to my car when a huge, powerful wind engulfed me leaving me unable to get to my car. If only I'd taken off those earmuffs, I could have prevented this.

The experience taught her that our angels and guides are always by our side. It's just that sometimes we tune them out. Once she learned to take off those spiritual earmuffs and recommitted herself to daily prayer and meditation, she underwent a profound spiritual awakening. She continues to help at her family-owned business, but today she also works as an intuitive reader and healer helping others connect with their angels.

It's important to note some common threads in these stories. The people in this chapter didn't receive their healing dreams the same night they asked for guidance. Like almost everything in life, it took some time. Don't give up if you're trying to work with your dreams and you're not receiving (or remembering) the dream guidance you seek. Give it time. In chapter 11, I'll give you some tips for remembering your dreams.

It's all a matter of maintaining focus over a specific period of time. Many experience their healing dreams as a result of their intent and focus. Where you direct your energy dictates the experiences you have—both during the day and at night while soul traveling in your dreams. If you intend to be healed or guided or led to answers, you will receive that healing, guidance, and insight as a result of your focused concentration.

I had a powerful dream when I was still in my "astral psychic dream school" that illustrates this point. In the dream, my guide led me to a clearing in a forest. I watched as a group of people stood in a circle. My guide told me they were meditating together trying to manage their anger. As I watched, their anger left their bodies and formed into a swirling red mass within the circle. Then the group focused on sending love and healing to this mass and it transformed into a ball of light and was absorbed back into their energy.

Then my guide led me to a circle of men and women who were working on erasing negative energy from the planet. I watched as an image of Earth hovered in the circle. As each of them sent energy to the globe, drops of negative energy dripped off it onto the ground. My guide said: "This is sustained focused energy work. Anyone can do this and use this form of meditation to manifest anything they want for their highest good. It's best done in groups."

As you learn to work with your energy, you too can create powerful transformational healing in your own life.

The meditation in this chapter's exercise is designed to help get you started on your healing journey.

## SENDING HEALING ENERGY

We are all powerful forces of energy. As children of our Creator, a spark from God exists in all of us—which means that we too can send healing energy. When you fall asleep praying for someone, your soul may travel to visit that person and offer help or healing. But you can also ask your angels and guides to send healing energy to a friend or loved one. I read years ago that Pope John Paul II fell asleep each night asking his guardian angel to talk to Ronald Reagan's angel and Mikhail Gorbachev's angel to bring about a resolution of the Cold War.

As a child, I had a hard time falling asleep and often ran to my parents' room. Dad would say: "If you wake up in the middle of the night, it means someone needs your prayers. Say an Our Father and a Hail Mary and you'll soon be fast asleep." Surprisingly, this suggestion worked. Each time I awoke, I lulled myself to sleep by saying prayers and visualizing them flying out through the bedroom window and landing in the heart of someone who needed comfort. After I shared this story on my podcast, a listener emailed to tell me about a spontaneous healing dream experience she shared with her roommate after trying this.

> I was having a hard time sleeping recently so
> I decided to try your suggestion of praying
> for someone in need of a prayer. Rather than

praying for someone specific, I started praying more generally for anyone who needed a prayer. I just kept repeating over and over that whoever needed healing or help in any way, that they would be blessed and healed. I woke up several times in the night and each time, I was able to fall back asleep by praying and sending healing to anyone who needed it. This was the first time I had tried this, and it proved to be very effective.

When I woke up in the morning, I was in the kitchen getting ready for work. My roommate came out of her room and said: "I had the most spiritually healing and powerful dreams last night." She started tearing up and talked about how she felt like so much profound spiritual healing was happening to her on a deep, energetic level and that all of these beings were coming to her to help her.

What are the odds that on the exact same night that I was trying out praying for someone else for the first time as a method for helping me sleep, that she had such a profound dream? I wonder if some of my prayers helped her with her healing. Either way, it was a special synchronicity. Sometimes I forget that prayers do make a difference, but whether it was my prayers or someone else's, I feel like this was a sign that sending love out into the world has a profound impact in ways that we can't even begin to comprehend or imagine.

Soon after this email, I received another from a listener:

I've been battling with depression for years and tried everything to combat this—meditation, yoga, medication, therapy. Nothing worked. On your podcast, you talk a lot about prayer. Since leaving the church years ago, I haven't prayed in a long time. In fact, I wasn't even sure I'd remember how to. But I figured, what have I got to lose? So I found my grandmother's old rosary beads in my jewelry box and began saying the Hail Mary. I couldn't remember the other prayers you're supposed to say, so I just said the Hail Mary over and over.

That night, I fell asleep feeling frustrated because the prayers didn't ease my anxiety at all. But then I dreamed that I was lying in my bed. I heard a lovely woman's voice say: "I am everyone's mother" and then I felt myself being lifted up out of the bed. Normally, this sensation would panic me, but in the dream, I just went with it.

I saw myself being placed in what I can only describe as a CAT scan, tube-like machine. As I lay in this machine, different colors washed over my body. It felt so peaceful and relaxing. I could hear this soothing music gently playing in the background, but it was like nothing I've heard before, so I don't have adequate words to describe it. Then I felt myself drifting back into my bed.

When I awoke in the morning, I felt happy for the first time in years. That dream was almost six months ago, and the heavy sadness has yet to return.

The power of dreams and prayer are truly miraculous when and if we allow ourselves to be transformed by them.

If you look for a pattern in these stories, you'll see that each dreamer was seeking something—either to send or receive healing. They were consistent with their requests and asked for help. Two key words when trying this yourself are "patience" and "consistency." For many of us, we have years of doubt and trust issues to work through before the power of healing can penetrate our aura. But with time and effort, combined with our repeated petitions, the help we seek to give or receive will manifest for each of us.

### Exercise: Akashic Records Meditation

As you lay down to fall asleep tonight, visualize yourself standing at the ocean's shore. The waves lap softly at your feet and the sun shines warmly upon your face. Take a deep breath, filling your lungs with the crisp, salty, fresh air. You feel relaxed and peaceful as your shoulders and neck drop, releasing all tension from your day. Your spine relaxes and sheds any extra energy you've been holding. This feeling of serenity and peace fills your stomach and drifts down into your hips, your thighs, your ankles, and your toes. Feel all your stress and tension drop away from your energy and slip into the healing waters before you.

As you gaze out at the ocean's horizon, you see a fluffy cloud descend from the sky and hover before you. Feeling relaxed and rejuvenated, you climb atop the cloud and allow it to take you up into the sky. As it floats higher and higher, you feel your energy getting lighter. Your vibrations lift, taking you to new heights of spiritual awareness. Floating on this cloud, you feel lighter than a feather and completely relaxed. If any worries intrude, visualize yourself tossing them off the cloud into the ocean far below you. The cloud continues to soar higher and higher into the sky. See yourself floating up and up and up until you're floating so high you realize you've reached the other side.

Suddenly, you see that you're floating above a beautiful crystal city. All the buildings are made of crystal that glitters in the warm sunlight. Peering over your cloud, you see a huge crystal building with tall columns and a massive stairway leading to large double doors. The cloud begins to descend, gently lowering you until you're standing at the top of these stairs and facing these doors.

You realize that you're standing outside the Hall of Records. Inside this building is a book. The *Book of You*. It stores everything your soul has ever done and experienced, and everything you plan to do. As you gently hop off the cloud, the giant double doors open to you, signifying that you're ready to enter. Take a moment as you walk through these doors to look around. Inside is the most intricate, elaborate, ornate library you've ever seen. Spiral staircases lead up to higher levels that hold more books. You feel the hushed, reverent silence of this sacred library as you begin looking for the *Book of You*.

As you walk through this mystical library, think of a question you'd like to know more about concerning your soul's purpose. You could ask: "What is my soul's purpose?" Or: "What is one thing that's holding me back right now?" Or: "What do I most need to know to further my spiritual development?"

As you meditate on your question, see yourself walking up one of the spiral staircases leading you to the book you seek. When you get to the top of the stairs, you feel compelled to walk down an aisle straight ahead knowing that your *Book of You* is in this aisle. Take a moment to walk down this aisle and find your sacred book. If your book is up high, simply ask for a stool and one will manifest for you.

Once you've found the *Book of You*, see yourself carrying it to a nearby desk. Before opening the book, say: "I ask permission to read my soul records to find the answer my soul needs." As you open the *Book of You*, allow yourself to be guided to the right page. Don't force this. Simply allow the book to flip to the page you need at this moment.

Take your time adjusting to the energy of the book. You may see words or a memory may jump out of the book. Be patient and allow the words, emotions, and imagery to appear for you. Your only job is to observe.

When you feel you've received the answer you seek, see yourself returning the book to its rightful home. As you walk out of the Hall of Records into the warm sunlight, your cloud awaits. Visualize yourself climbing atop the cloud and resuming your journey through the skies. But this time, you feel yourself descending—down, down, and down. Feel your spirit coming back into your body as the cloud gently floats down through the sky, past other clouds, over the ocean, before depositing you back on the shore.

When you feel ready, flutter your eyes open and write down your thoughts, impressions, and feelings in your dream journal. Before falling asleep tonight repeat: "I am open to receiving healing guidance in my dreams."

# Chapter 7

# LUCID DREAMS

*Hidden within your dreams there is a precious jewel,
a treasure of incalculable value if you were to find
it. But to find it, you must first master the power of
being awake in your dreams.*

Stephen LaBerge

Lucid dreaming is the state of being aware of yourself dreaming *while* you're dreaming. Though most people report having had at least one lucid dream, only about 20 percent of the population report having lucid dreams on a regular basis. This number is growing, however, as more and more people start to learn techniques that help them to become lucid in their dreams. Stephen LaBerge, a pioneer researcher in this field and author of the groundbreaking book *Lucid Dreaming: The Power of Being Awake and Aware in Your Dreams*, says that lucid dreamers are able to confront nightmares, heal inner conflicts, and achieve an enlightened awareness that can lead to profound peace.

So much of our lives is lived unconsciously. We take the same route to and from work or school each day, often without even being conscious of the drive. How many times have you arrived at work and wondered: "How'd I get here?" You were functioning on autopilot. If you don't resist this tendency, you can let whole years slip by, leaving you to lament: "How'd I get here? I don't like my job. I can't wait to retire. This isn't the life I planned."

When I taught English, I started each semester by telling my students this famous story about Ernest Hemingway. One day while sitting at a bar, a friend challenged him to write a short story using just six words. Hemingway accepted the challenge and wrote: "Baby shoes for sale. Never worn." Then I'd tell my students to write their life story in six words or less and come back the next week to share it with the class. One student returned the following week and shared this story: "Work, work more. Rinse and repeat." That was twenty years ago, but I never forgot that student or the sad, dejected way he shared his "life story." I think many of us can empathize with him, because there are times when life does feel like nothing more than "work, pay bills, sleep, work again."

Yet when we learn to work with the unconscious mind—kneading it like dough to find nuggets of truth waiting to rise to the surface—our unconscious inner self suddenly aligns with our consciousness. We're awake. We're alive, truly alive, and living our authentic truth. When we learn to practice lucid dreaming, we begin to recognize that we're co-creators of our waking and dreaming lives. The walls come down. The barriers between you and me, us and them, this world and the next—they dissolve.

There are levels of lucid dreaming. If you know you're dreaming just as you're coming out of a dream, that's one aspect of lucid dreaming. But true lucid dreaming involves being aware of dreaming *while you're in the dream.* Once lucid in a dream, you can manifest your thoughts, create anything from your intentions, confront your shadow side, heal conflicts with people in your life, or find creative solutions to problems.

Christopher Nolan wrote *Inception* after experimenting with lucid dreaming. This psychological thriller is about people who can enter the dreams of others. Nolan said: "I wrote the first draft of this script seven or eight years ago, but it goes back much further, this idea of approaching the dream life as another state of reality." Richard Linklater's work, especially his movie *Waking Life*, was also inspired by his lucid dreams. "I never really thought about it much," he says, "but these dreams would happen, and I would be aware I was in a dream. As I started to make this movie, I started doing all the research, I knew it had to be a phenomenon, and it confirmed a lot of my own experience."

## AWAKENING TO YOUR DREAMS

For many people, lucid dreams are preceded by a spiritual awakening. As you learn to transcend your conscious, waking mind during the day, this transfers to your dreaming world, allowing you to soar to new heights of spiritual development. Setting the intention to have a lucid dream has also been shown to trigger one. Simply reading this book, and others on dreams and lucid dreaming in particular, will signal your unconscious mind to retain lucidity in the dream state.

Lucid dreams have been written about for thousands of years. One of the most fascinating early reports of a lucid dream was recounted by Saint Augustine in a letter he wrote in 415 AD. In his letter, he writes about a series of profound lucid dreams experienced by his friend Gennadius, a physician from Carthage who often struggled with his faith and the concept of an eternal life after death. He told Augustine that, one night, he dreamed he saw a beautiful man with a "commanding presence" who told him to follow him. As in all lucid dreams, in this experience, Gennadius was aware of all his senses. He writes about hearing beautiful music and seeing vivid colors. He awoke from this experience and thought it was just a lovely dream.

But the next night, the commanding young man appeared once again in his dream and asked Gennadius if he recognized him. The doctor replied that he remembered meeting the angelic young man in his dream the night before. The young man then asked Gennadius if they had met in his dreams or in his waking life. Gennadius said: "In sleep." The young man seemed pleased with this response, saying: "You remember it well; it is true that you saw these things in sleep, but I would have you know that even now you are seeing in sleep." Then the two shared an intriguing exchange:

"Where is your body now?" the heavenly guide asked.

Gennadius said, "In my bed."

"Do you know that the eyes in this body of yours are now bound and closed, and that with these eyes you are seeing nothing?"

"I know it," said Gennadius.

"What then are the eyes with which you see me? As while you are asleep and lying on your bed these eyes of your body are now unemployed and do nothing, and yet you have eyes with which you behold me, and enjoy this vision, so, after your death, while your bodily eyes shall be wholly inactive, there shall be in you a life by which you shall still live, and a faculty of perception by which you shall still perceive. Beware, therefore, after this of harboring doubts as to whether the life of man shall continue after his death."

Tibetan Buddhists also taught lucid dreaming through yogic practices centuries before this. Called "dream yoga," this technique is included in the *Six Doctrines or Truths*. In the twelfth century, the Sufi teacher Ibn El-Arabi is said to have told his students: "A person must control his thoughts in a dream. The training of this alertness will produce great benefits for the individual." Tantric books from India also teach lucid dreaming.

Twentieth-century psychiatrist Nathan Rapport wrote about a technique that helped him have more lucid dreams.

As he was falling asleep each night, he made a mental note of his day and then, as he entered the hypnagogic state, he made a mental note of all the images flashing in his mind. This "inquisitive attention," he believed, enhanced his chances of becoming lucid in his dreams. But it's probably the work of Stephen LaBerge in his Stanford University research lab that brought lucid dreaming into the mainstream and encouraged people to take it seriously.

LaBerge has dedicated his life to lucid-dreaming research. He argues that, if we spend a third of our life sleeping, why should we waste it by being unconscious? LaBerge believes that lucid dreamers have richer, more enlightened lives full of profound experiences that enable them to tackle problems, travel the world (and even the dimensions), and defy known physical laws—like flying and walking through walls.

I have a recurring dream that I am standing in front of my guide, who tells me to flap my arms. As I do so in the dream, I begin to fly. In these dreams, I am always aware that this is a dream, but I decide to go with it because it feels so liberating to fly up and away to anywhere I want to go. This is a key aspect of maintaining lucidity in a dream. If you become frightened or startled as you recognize that you're dreaming, you will most likely awaken from the lucid dream. It's important to maintain a "go with the flow" attitude in lucid dreams.

Lucid-dream research also teaches that people who tend to be creative have more lucid dreams, as do those who meditate on a regular basis. Vivid sounds, colors, sights, and sensations are hallmarks of a lucid dream. Some people report feeling a tingling sensation running through their bodies, as if their vibrations are running at a higher level than normal. Their emotions seem to be heightened as well. You may even experience intense joy, anger, or sadness, or even spiritual ecstasy, in a lucid dream.

Lucid dreaming is not the same as astral travel, however. We'll discuss out-of-body experiences, or astral travel, in the next chapter. Even though these are similar experiences, lucid dreaming is said to occur in the imagination, whereas astral travel involves your soul actually leaving your body to explore other places.

Physicist Fred Alan Wolf believes that lucid dreams belong in the realm of parallel universes and calls lucid dreaming "parallel universe awareness." But while we can't be sure exactly where we go when we lucid dream, what we do know is that lucid dreams enable us to journey within to the core of our hidden selves. We can wrestle with our inner conflicts, overcome fears and inhibitions, receive creative insights, and gain foresight as we become one with our unconscious awareness.

In all of my soul travels—dreams in which I am giving readings, receiving guidance from higher beings, or meeting with loved ones on the other side—I am always aware that I am in a dream state. These dreams have an intensity to them, as if my guides are saying: "Pay attention! This is important." Many of the dreams reported by experienced lucid dreamers even have an *Alice in Wonderland* quality to them, manifesting strange characters at will or creating a new world to play in. Rosemary Ellen Guiley writes about sitting atop a lighthouse and dancing a ballet with herself in lucid dreams. LaBerge writes about having sex in his lucid dreams. Some have lucid dreams in which animals talk to them. Others have lucid dreams that foretell the future or help them with specific challenges in their lives.

A listener to my podcast shared a lucid dream that helped her overcome stage fright. She'd just published an important research paper and the university where she taught wanted her to present it. In her dream, she was walking through a crowded auditorium. As everyone was pushing her onto the stage, she suddenly realized she was dreaming.

> Then, as I walked on the stage, everyone turned into huge rabbits. They all started laughing. It was as though we were all in on this cosmic joke together. I started to laugh too realizing I was dreaming this ridiculous dream. When I woke up, I was still laughing. I thought to myself: "Your presentation is nothing in the scheme of life. Just get up there, share your research and try to make them laugh." I did just that, and now I am being asked to give my talk at universities and colleges up and down the West Coast.

When I read her story, it reminded me of a vivid lucid dream I had a few years ago. I was in a large workshop that reminded me of something children might imagine if you asked them to visualize Santa's workshop. There were worktables built into the richly carved mahogany walls, which were at least forty feet high with thirty-foot-high windows. Each window overlooked a different scene. One displayed a wintry scene with snow-topped mountains. Another looked out onto a green valley with wildflowers scattered over the emerald grass. Through a third, I saw the ocean with water as clear as glass, while the fourth framed a scene that included a lush forest with mile-high oaks and pine trees. As I took in the vivid and distinctly different imagery that greeted me from each window, I realized I was dreaming.

Just then I felt the presence of a tall man standing behind me to my right. I never turned to stare at him, but instead allowed him to guide me gently to one of the worktables. Everything in this dream was so massive that I had to stand on a ladder so I could see what he was trying to show me. On the table, there were hundreds of what I can only describe as snow globes. The man told me to look carefully at each one. Inside each globe was a whole world. One was Earth. Some of the others were different versions of Earth. I could see planes, cars, people going to work, cities, and countrysides. In one, there was a whole world in which everything was pink, orange, and yellow. Pink mountains, orange water, and yellow land. The man stood behind me watching me take it all in, then he said: "I created all these illusions. Choose your illusion." I nodded slowly and considered carefully before I saw myself jumping into one of the globes. Then I woke up.

# THE ILLUSION OF SEPARATENESS

It's important to note that, after this dream, in my dream journal, I wrote: "I saw myself jump into" one of the globes. This is a key aspect of lucid dreaming, in which the dreamer is both the participant and the observer. LaBerge writes that, in lucid dreams, we are often the observer and the participant at the same time. For example, if you dream that you are watching someone dance on a stage, you may suddenly then find yourself in the awareness (or consciousness) of the dancer. He writes:

> Which of these states of identification characterizes the lucid dreamer—participant or observer? The answer is a combination of both. The combination of these two perspectives is characteristic of lucid dreaming and allows the lucid dreamer to be in the dream but not of it.

This feeling of being both participant and observer melts away the illusion of separateness that often divides us. As Taoist philosopher and teacher Chuang Tzu wrote:

> One night I dreamt I was a butterfly, fluttering here and there, content with my lot. Suddenly I awoke, and I was Chuang Tzu again. Who am I in reality? A butterfly dreaming that I am Chuang Tzu, or Chuang Tzu dreaming he was a butterfly?

In addition to being both participant and observer, lucid dreamers often encounter universal archetypes. One client shared a lucid dream with me that occurred when he was looking for his first job after graduation. He had the qualifications, but didn't feel he was performing well on the interviews. He had a lucid dream in which his dad was yelling at him, telling him that he was no good and would never get hired. "Suddenly," he recalls, "my dad got bigger and bigger as he's screaming at me."

> In the dream, I wasn't frightened because I knew I was dreaming. I was both watching myself stare at my dad grow into a giant, and I was also the little me kid sitting there letting my dad berate me. As my dad beefs up into this huge giant, I watch as little me casually slips a sling shot out of my back pocket. Just like I was David fighting Goliath, I aim the sling shot at my giant dad's head. Suddenly, my dad morphs into me. This whole time my dad/me are yelling horrible insults at me. I never had to shoot the sling shot, though, because as soon as the giant dad turned into me, I dropped the sling shot and hugged myself.

This dream helped him realize that he was still carrying his dad's rage inside himself. He began working to heal his inner child through self-love, meditation, and affirmation, and he got the job he wanted within three months of his lucid dream.

So what is actually happening when we lucid dream? Are we traveling to parallel dimensions or are we simply awake and aware in our own imaginations? While the jury is still out on that question, science is starting to turn up some fascinating research on what happens to our physical bodies while we're dreaming. In a 2009 study, sleep researchers Ursula Voss, Romain Holzmann, and J. Allan Hobson were able to demonstrate significant differences in the electrophysiology of the frontal lobe in lucid dreamers as compared to non-lucid sleep. As they reported in *Sleep Journal:* "Our data show that lucid dreaming constitutes a hybrid state of consciousness with definable and measurable differences from waking and from REM sleep, particularly in frontal areas."

How did they know when a participant in the study was lucid dreaming? The answer to that question brings us back to the work of Stephen LaBerge. In 1978, LaBerge wanted to discover a way to signal his research team that he was lucid dreaming, hoping to discover when we typically lucid dream—during REM or Delta sleep. But since our bodies are partially paralyzed when we sleep, the problem was how he could communicate his lucid dreaming awareness to his team. Then inspiration hit him. Since we can move our eyes during REM and deep sleep, he could signal with his eyes. The team agreed that LaBerge would move his eyes in a predetermined pattern to indicate that he was having a lucid dream. Since Laberge's breakthrough, sleep researchers have used this technique to greatly advance our knowledge of lucid dreaming.

## HELPFUL TECHNIQUES

There are several techniques you can use to enhance your ability to dream lucidly and to increase the number of lucid dreams you experience. LaBerge created a technique called MILD—Mnemonic Induction of Lucid Dreams—as a memory aid to help dreamers become more proficient at lucid dreaming. He recommends that, upon waking each morning, you don't move or jump out of bed. Simply stay still and go over the last dream you recall. Go over this dream several times until you've committed it to memory. Then try to fall back asleep while telling yourself that you will remember to recognize that you're dreaming. As you're falling asleep, visualize yourself back in the dream you've just remembered. Repeat these two steps—telling yourself you'll remember to be aware in the dream and going over the dream you just had—until you fall back asleep.

Obviously, it's best to try this on a weekend when you can sleep in. LaBerge reminds us:

> In a night when you get seven hours of sleep, fifty percent of your dreaming time will fall in the last two hours. If you can afford to sleep an extra hour, it will be almost all dreaming time. So if you want to cultivate your dream life, you will have to find a way to sleep late—at least on weekends.

Another technique that has shown some success at encouraging lucid dreaming is the WILD method—Wake-Induced Lucid Dreams. This technique involves four steps:

- Lie down in your bed with your eyes closed. Relax your mind and body through meditation or guided visualization.

- Observe your hypnagogic state. Once you're relaxed, concentrate on the darkness behind your closed eyes and let your mind wander. Allow your mind to follow any images that appear in your mind's eye.

- Create the dream scene. Focus on what you want to dream about and create the scene to support this image.

- Sense when your mind is awake, but your body is asleep. Lucid dreaming occurs most often when the body is asleep (sleep paralysis) and the mind is awake. Allow yourself to linger as long as possible in this liminal state.

Another simple way to induce a lucid dream is to count backward from one hundred, repeating between the numbers: "I'm going to have a lucid dream" or "I will remember my dreams." Or perhaps try the more traditional Third-Eye Method, also called the chakra technique. This method involves focusing on your third-eye chakra, the space between and slightly above your eyebrows. With your eyes closed, stare forward and up at your third eye. This technique helps to open your third-eye chakra, the center of intuition and imagination. Opening this chakra has been known to enhance lucid dreaming.

A technique called the Wake Back to Bed technique is also very effective, but can be hard for people who have a difficult time falling asleep. It entails setting an alarm and waking yourself up after four to six hours of sleep so that you intentionally interrupt your REM sleep. This increases the odds of remembering your dream and/or becoming lucid when you fall back to sleep. As you're falling back to sleep, employ LaBerge's MILD method to further increase the likelihood of having a lucid dream.

To become a lucid dreamer, you must learn how to remember your dreams more vividly (see chapter 11). In fact, LaBerge believes that the two essential requirements for learning lucid dreaming are motivation and good dream recall. Without focused, prolonged intent and motivation, you can't learn to be lucid in your dreams. There's no such thing as instant anything. You can't lose weight instantly or get into shape overnight. And you won't be able to heal your inner child or awaken your intuition with the snap of your fingers either. Everything that is worthwhile takes time. But with patience, practice, motivation, and focused intent on remembering your dreams and becoming lucid while dreaming, it will happen for you.

**Exercise: Lucid Dreaming**
Listen to a guided meditation as you fall asleep, preferably one with binaural beats that work by sending a different frequency into each ear, forcing the brain to produce a third frequency. For example, if a 310 Hz sound is sent to the left ear, and a 315 Hz sound to the right ear, the brain will process and interpret the two frequencies as one 5 Hz frequency. The brain then creates a new brain wave at this frequency. This is only effective through headphones.

Once you've entered a relaxed state, stare at the darkness behind your closed eyes. Gently look up into your third-eye chakra and allow yourself to enter into a hypnagogic state. Become an observer of any images or thoughts that float through your mind.

Visualize the dream you'd like to enter. Engage all your senses. See the image. Hear the sounds associated with the dream. Smell any scents connected to the place. Allow yourself to feel the sun on your face, for example, or the breeze brushing past you. Try to visualize a goal you're currently working on, because this will help strengthen your manifesting intentions and your chances of lucid dreaming. If you're working on launching a new product at work, for example, lie in bed visualizing yourself presenting this product to your team. See everyone smiling and nodding in agreement. Visualize yourself signing a contract and shaking hands. Engage all your senses to reinforce and charge this image with your energy.

Continue this visualization until you fall asleep.

Upon waking, don't move a muscle. Force yourself to lie very still and allow any dream recollections to settle into your conscious memory. Go over the dream you remember best until you've committed it to memory. If you have time, try falling back asleep with the intention of re-entering this dream. Write down everything you can remember from the dream(s).

# Chapter 8

# ASTRAL TRAVEL

*I have wandered a long time through the world,*
*seeking those like you who sit upon a high tower on*
*the lookout for things unseen.*

Carl Jung

Astral travel is a method of projecting your soul out of your body to journey into other realms. Our physical bodies are enveloped in an astral body. Often called the second body or etheric double, this body contains subtle matter that can't be seen with our physical eyes. Everyone has an astral body, although this astral body is not the soul. It's the "vehicle of the soul," as British author Hereward Carrington points out in *The Projection of the Astral Body.*

During sleep, hypnosis, trance, anesthesia, or another unconscious state, our souls travel in this astral vehicle. Often severe trauma or pain can cause a spontaneous out-of-body experience. Think of those who've been in car accidents or were victims of crime who have reported that it was as if they were outside their bodies watching it happen.

When my mom was a little girl, she fell from a tree and dislocated her shoulder. As she lay in bed waiting for the doctor, she said the pain was so unbearable that she kept popping out of her body.

> Just as the pain became overwhelming, I found myself hovering near the ceiling looking down at myself. Each time, it scared me, and I'd drop back down into my body. But then the next wave of pain would hit me and I'd be back out of the body.

This does not mean, however, that you have to wait for a traumatic experience to try astral travel. Anyone can learn this technique through meditation exercises.

## SOUL JOURNEYS

Astral travel is an ancient skill that's been practiced by many throughout history and across cultures. The ancient Egyptians taught about the *ka,* which is not unlike what we think of today as the astral body. The ka is not the soul, but rather the vehicle by which Egyptians traveled to the other side. They often depicted this as a human body with a bird's head, possibly to indicate the ka's ability to fly. *The Tibetan Book of the Dead* teaches about a *bardo* body that is "endowed with all sense facilities" and has the power of "miraculous motion." Plato taught his students that the soul could travel outside of the body, and many mystics, saints, and healers have described leaving their bodies.

When we travel in the astral realm, we often look just as we do in our waking life, although some report seeing themselves as ghostly, transparent figures and some say they're invisible in this state of being, but that others can sense their presence. Sometimes when we travel out of the body, we're seen as points of light or energy that are felt rather than seen. These accounts of astral travelers appearing as transparent beings or points of light may account for some of the ghost stories and orb sightings we hear about.

When I was in middle school, I read Lois Duncan's *Stranger With My Face,* a book about twins who were separated at birth. They both learned to astral project and one twin took over the other, leaving her lost in a terrifying astral dimension. The book scared me and prevented me from trying hypnosis or meditation for the next several years. More recently, the show *Behind Her Eyes* has presented a similar frightening aspect of astral travel.

Nonetheless, research has shown that we are safe and protected by a silver cord when we go out of the body. This cord acts like an umbilical cord, tethering our astral selves to our physical bodies, and is only severed at the time of our death. Many claim that this cord is connected to the solar plexus chakra, which is located slightly above the navel, but American esoterisist Sulvane Muldoon, who wrote one of the first comprehensive books on astral travel (*Projections of the Astral Body,* 1929), says the cord is connected to the third-eye chakra, which is located between and slightly above the eyebrows.

There are two types of astral travel: spontaneous and experiential. Spontaneous astral travel can occur whenever we are unconscious—for instance, when we're dreaming, when we experience trauma, or when we are under anesthesia or in deep hypnosis. Experiential astral travel usually occurs after years of lucid dreaming or meditative practices. Oliver Fox, an electrical engineer and occultist, had his first experiential astral journey after fourteen years of trying to get out of his body. Robert Monroe, who founded the Monroe Institute in Virginia, developed a technique called hemi-sync that helps astral travelers achieve this effect much sooner. This technique, mentioned in the last chapter, introduces a different frequency into each ear, thereby producing a third frequency that is said to help induce astral travel.

Parapsychologist Charles Tart lists five important characteritics of traditional out-of-body experiences. He says they are universal, in that they have been reported throughout history and across cultures. They tend to be "once in a lifetime" occurrences often precipitated by illness or profound emotional stress. They are life-changing, causing many to feel at one with the Universe and have a deep understanding of this life and the afterlife. They are, on average, positive experiences and their details can later be verified as actually having happened at the time of the experience.

A common theme among astral travelers is the need to cultivate a spiritual mindset. Overcoming our fears of leaving our physical bodies and increasing our meditative practices builds the foundation for a healthy astral experience. In *Dreams and Premonitions*, famed theosophist L. W. Rogers claims that people with lower vibrations—either due to stress, depression, or illness—tend to stay close to their bodies during sleep. But people with higher vibrations—from living a balanced, healthy life and practicing meditation—tend to travel to the astral planes during sleep.

Thus astral travel seems to take lucid dreaming to a whole new level. In addition to being awake and aware in the "dream state," astral travelers are conscious of being out of their bodies and in a different location. Many people have reported and verified these astral journeys. Here are just a few.

## ROBERT MONROE

Robert Monroe, a Virginia businessman, began having spontaneous out-of-body experiences in the late 1950s and wrote about them extensively in his book *Journeys Out of the Body: The Classic Work on Out-of-Body Experience*. His journeys began on a quiet Sunday afternoon while his family was at church. When he lay down for a nap, a beam of light that came from no identifiable source poured into the room and lit up his body. He reports that his whole body began to shake and vibrate, even though his physical body didn't move. This occurrence repeated itself several times over the next two months. At first, he thought he might be having seizures. But then he reminded himself that, even though it felt as if his body were shaking, in reality it wasn't.

After getting a clean bill of health from his doctor, Monroe decided that the next time he had this vibrating feeling, he would simply surrender to it and see what happened. He forced himself to relax into the strange sensation, which he described as an electric shock moving through his body without the pain of electrocution. He also saw what looked like a ring of light that circled his body from head to toe before spinning back to his head.

One night, as he lay on his stomach with his hand hanging off the bed, brushing the top of the rug, the vibrating sensation started tingling through his body once again. This time, he tried to move through it and extended his hand through the rug into the floor below. He felt the pipes there and grabbed on to a triangular piece of wood located between his bedroom floor and the ceiling of the room below. The shock of this brought Monroe back to his body. Nonetheless, he continued his attempts to leave his body and eventually found himself traveling to friends' homes, where he was able to verify the things and people he saw there.

Monroe also used his astral travels to journey to other dimensions. His experiences led him to create the Monroe Institute, which is still thriving today. People can go there for training and to learn how to work with their consciousness to achieve astral travel, enhance their psychic abilities, and deepen their intuition. His work became so highly regarded that even the U. S. Army sent an officer to his institute to look into his work and report on it. After undertaking a seven-day course in the use of hemi-sync-induced hypnosis to expand consciousness, one officer said that, if our consciousness were a lamp, then the hypnotized consciousness was a laser beam. So the army set about recruiting officers who showed an aptitude for intuition and had open minds. Eventually, over thirty officers were chosen and taught how to hypnotize themselves to induce out-of-body experiences. Their work with remote viewing led to many successful rescues and discoveries. (For more information on this topic, check out Russell Targ, Dale Graff, and Stephen Schwartz.)

Monroe describes three general locations on the other side. The first includes people and places that exist here in our physical world. The second includes heaven and hell, where we connect with our deceased loved ones. At the higher levels here, he encountered more heavenly and benevolent beings. At the lower levels, which he describes as being closer to our earthly dimension, he encountered scary and negative entities. The third location exists outside of our space/time continuum and contains parallel universes. Monroe claimed that, beyond these locales, there were many more dimensions that he was unable to visit because they were beyond his conscious capabilities.

As a medium, I've often come across this idea of multiple levels and dimensions. Apparently, the more advanced your soul is, the higher the level you can achieve. It's not unlike a school here on the physical plane. A kindergartner, for example, isn't able to comprehend a high school English class, just as an eighth grader would be lost in a graduate-level physics class. Perhaps, as our souls advance, we will be able to explore these higher dimensions.

## OLIVER FOX

Hugh Callaway (1885–1949), short-story writer, poet, and occultist, lived in a time when the mysteries of astral travel were still considered odd at best, or a mark of insanity at worst. This forced him to write his works on astral travel under the pseudonym Oliver Fox. He first began his astral travels through his lucid dreaming, which demonstrates how we can transition from dreamers to experiencers. When we learn how to recall our dreams, we can evolve into lucid dreamers and finally be transformed into astral travelers.

After years of working with lucid dreaming, Fox finally discovered a way to leave his body. By concentrating on the pineal gland (located behind the third-eye chakra) and willing himself to push through what he called the "pineal door," he claimed he was able to project himself out of his physical body. Once outside his body he, like Monroe, saw a golden light that was so bright "it seemed the whole room burst into flame." Fox claimed that we are all clairvoyant and clairaudient in this astral state and, again like Monroe, described feeling a vibratory sensation while in a hypnagogic state between waking and sleeping that was often accompanied by pain and fear.

Could this explain sleep paralysis? Is it possible that, when we wake to find ourselves in this liminal stage between sleep and waking, the fear and pressure we feel isn't "an old hag" sitting atop our chests, but rather our astral bodies trying to push themselves out of their physical home? Fox seems to indicate that it is:

> I felt as though I were rushing to insanity and death; but once the little door clicked behind

me, I enjoyed mental clarity far surpassing that of Earth life. And the fear was gone. Leaving the body was then as easy as getting out of bed.

Others have found different methods for achieving astral travel. Journalist D. Scott Rogo visualizes himself in a car driving at high speed down a steep hill and feels himself pulling out of the body—out of the car—just as it crashes. "Since many OBEs are reported on the verge of sleep," he writes, "by controlling this state of consciousness, one can more readily direct the OBE than at any other time." Other astral travelers visualize their souls shrinking to a point of light and then emerging out of the top of their heads.

Fox wrote often about the difficulty of sustaining his energy during his astral journeys. "The mental process of prolonging the dream produced a pain in the pineal gland," he reports, "dull at first but rapidly increasing in intensity. I knew intuitively this was a warning to no longer resist the call of my body." This statement really stood out to me because, when I started doing readings, I noticed that, after four hours, my forehead started to throb. Not really a headache, but rather as if my third eye were crying out in pain for rest. When I am doing readings, time melts away. I am usually unaware of anything going on around me as I focus on the information coming through from the other side. When intuitives are in this alternate state of awareness, we are, in a way, unconsciously projecting our astral bodies to the other side so we can receive information and act as literal mediums between the two worlds.

While Monroe wrote extensively about the frightening entities he encountered in what he called Locale II, Fox never reported seeing anything scary on the astral plane. The scenery for him just looked like earthly locales. He was usually invisible to others, but if others did see him, they reacted in shock and fear, as if they were seeing a ghost. Their fearful reaction often startled Fox as well and sent him immediately back into his physical body.

Fox's description of this startled reaction reminds me of the first time I saw an apparition. My mom and I were preparing to head out for a shopping trip when she asked me to run upstairs to her room and get her purse. I sprinted up the stairs, intent on grabbing the purse and heading back down, but when I ran into my parents' room, I saw an elderly gentleman standing in my mother's open closet doorway. I was shocked because he was not a typical see-through apparition. He appeared to be disoriented and confused. When I gasped loudly, he turned and focused on me. Then he gasped as well and disappeared. The following week, my grandmother died unexpectedly from a stroke. When we went through her belongings, I found a picture of her father. It was the man I'd seen in my parents' bedroom.

Monroe and Fox both emphasize in their work that time is a created concept, arguing that there is no time in the astral dimensions. Everything is *now*. A paranormal investigator once told me a fascinating story about an alleged haunted house he was called to investigate. An elderly woman answered the door and told him her house was haunted by noisy children. Sometimes she saw them running through the kitchen laughing or leaving the cabinet doors open. Sometimes she heard them playing in the backyard. The children weren't mean or scary, she said, but they still frightened her and she wanted them gone. The investigator found only a few faint traces of children laughing and playing, but he returned to the house periodically to check on the woman. Each time, she reported that she was still plagued by the ghostly children.

Years later, when the investigator returned to check on the woman again, a young mother answered the door. She explained that they'd recently moved in after the previous owner had died. When the investigator explained why he was there, the young mother's face went pale. "But that's so strange," she said finally. "My children talk about seeing the ghostly apparition of an elderly woman sitting in the living room." The investigator was shocked. Perhaps this was no haunting at all, but rather a mysterious time loop where the future was bumping into the past. As he left, he heard the mother call to her children: "Kids! Stop leaving these kitchen cabinet doors open!"

## SYLVAN MULDOON

Sylvan Muldoon, an early 20th-century esotericist, wrote a fascinating account of his astral travels in his book *Projections of the Astral Body*. His first out-of-body experience occurred when he was twelve. He and his family were visiting a Spiritualist center, staying at a hotel with a dozen other mediums. This is important, because it indicates he had an open mind about esoteric concepts and a natural appreciation for intuitive thought, two fundamental requirements for astral travel.

It is also true that mediums tend to get better results when working in the presence of other intuitives, who may provide additional power to their readings. This is why we tend to get better results in spiritual séances or meditation circles than when we work alone. Muldoon believes that having all those mediums in one building served to fire up his natural intuitive ability and helped pave the way for his first astral journey.

On the evening in question, Muldoon went to bed around 10:30, but woke a few hours later in a state of sleep paralysis. His whole body began to vibrate and he felt immense pressure in the back of his head. He found himself floating above his rigid body and, in the next moment, he was standing upright next to his bed. A cord that he described as "an elastic-like cable" connected the back of his astral head to the forehead of his physical body right at the third-eye chakra. He tried to leave his bedroom to get help but, when he tried to turn the doorhandle, he was shocked to discover that he simply passed through the locked, closed door. After finding that he was unable to make his presence known to anyone, he felt a tugging sensation on the cord and was soon back in his body.

Muldoon observed that the energy cord connecting his astral and physical bodies was attached to the medulla oblongata, "which has direct control over the organs of respiration in the physical body." He also claimed that flying and falling dreams are what the conscious mind remembers from the unconscious astral projection of the body.

Muldoon called this astral somnambulism "unconscious astral projection," writing that "during sleep, many mediums travel in the astral body but never become conscious while doing so." This made me wonder whether this is what my soul-travel dreams are. In my astral dream experiences, I do feel conscious of who I am and what I am doing, but I wouldn't call it lucid dreaming because, in these "dreams," I am aware that I'm somewhere else doing the work I came here to do. Could it be that when we dream of loved ones in heaven, we're actually astral traveling to them?

Muldoon believes that everyone travels to the astral planes while asleep. William Walker Anderson, who wrote on this topic at the turn of the 20th century, claims:

> In the case of dreams, the astral body may become detached and sent on long journeys, travelling at a rate of speed only less than that of light waves. The jumbled recollections of these dreams are occasioned by the brain not having received perfect impressions transmitted to it, by reason or lack of training and development—the result being like a distorted photograph.

This means that, as we all work to raise our consciousness through intuitive development, meditation, and prayer, we not only begin to remember our dreams more clearly, but also start to recall our spontaneous astral somnambulism more clearly as well.


## THE LADY IN BLUE

One of the most famous cases of an out-of-body experience occurred in the 17th century. Sister Maria de Jesus was born to a wealthy, pious family in Agreda, Spain. Her parents said she began speaking to invisible friends at the age of four. They described her as a calm, reasonable, and highly spiritual young girl who expressed a compassionate desire to help the poor. When Maria was twelve, she announced to her family that she was joining a convent so she could devote her life to God. Shortly before her big send off, however, her mother had a powerful, mystical experience in which she claimed that the voice of God commanded that she and her husband convert their castle into a convent devoted to helping the poor and that she and her daughters take their vows at the newly established convent. The men in the family, she claimed, were to join the local monastery. She and her husband sold all their belongings and the whole family devoted their lives to God.

When Maria was eighteen, she was kneeling in the convent church praying when she found herself slipping into a trance. Before she knew what was happening, she saw herself standing in front of people from the American Southwest. Somehow, she was able to speak their language and her astral body was able to carry physical rosary beads to give to those she encountered. Maria began teaching these people about God, the Bible, and Christian doctrine.

Eventually, she told all of this to her confessor, who reported it to the archbishop. The archbishop was shocked to read about a young nun who'd never left Spain and yet was telling tales of teaching the gospels to groups of people she called "the Titas" and "the Jumanos." Intrigued yet still skeptical, he wrote to ask his missionaries in what is now New Mexico, Arizona, and Texas whether they'd heard of a young woman appearing to people in the area.

Father Benavides, who'd been a missionary in the Southwest for years, answered that he had no idea what the archbishop was talking about. Shortly thereafter, however, a delegation of Jumanos arrived to talk to him about a beautiful lady dressed in blue robes "who comes from the sky" to heal the sick, hand out rosary beads, and teach them about Christianity. They said she had instructed them to ask Father Benavides to send missionaries to them so they could learn more.

Father Benavides and several other priests followed the delegates back home to check out the story for themselves. On the way, they met twelve chiefs who were waiting to escort them the rest of the way. When Father Benavides asked the chiefs how they'd known to arrive at that precise time to meet them, they said the Lady in Blue had told them. The priests were shocked to find thousands of people waiting for them when they arrived, all knowledgeable about Christian doctrine. The priests spent the next several days baptizing anyone who wanted to be baptized, and many miraculous healings were reported over these days.

When Father Benavides later traveled to Spain to meet this famous Lady in Blue, she recognized him instantly and said that she had been with him in spirit when he was baptizing the people. She also told him of the various places and people she'd visited in her astral travels in the past decade and some of the names and back stories of the Jumanos and Tejas with whom Father Benavides had met.

Maria was questioned twice by the Spanish Inquisition, but they could never prove that she was lying. Dozens of highly placed people—including the archbishop and Father Benavides—testified to the veracity of her story, and some of her fellow sisters reported that they had seen her levitating while in a trance state. King Felipe IV called on her for counsel and continued to meet with her for spiritual guidance for twenty years. Maria, who was also a medium, passed on messages of validation and comfort to the king from his deceased son, Baltasar Carlos.

Maria claimed to have met often with Mother Mary, who asked her to write her autobiography. Maria wrote 400 pages of Mother Mary's life in just twenty days. The writings are still in print today and comprise a six-volume work called *The Mystical City of God*. The book contains information that was unknown to the world at that time, like the fact that the Earth is round and what it looks like from space. Maria made one last astral visit to the Jumanos before her death to say goodbye. The next morning, the Jumanos found the hillside where she'd appeared covered with bluebonnet flowers.

There are dozens more stories just like Sister Maria's. Padre Pio, a mystical saint from Italy who received the stigmata of Christ in 1910, was known to appear in two places at the same time. Dozens of witnesses reported that he was celebrating Mass on a certain day at a time when other credible witnesses claimed to have seen him in a different part of the world offering healings. Saint Martin de Porres, Saint John Bosco, Saint Anthony of Padua, Saint Ambrose of Milan, and Saint Isadore de Labrador were all known to bi-locate as well. Perhaps this is another form of astral travel.

One priest told me that the Bible doesn't condemn astral travel. In fact, the Franciscans teach that it's a vehicle for the Holy Spirit to commune with mystics and saints. While I agree with this, I do not feel that astral travel is reserved for a few chosen saintly people. Robert Monroe wasn't a believer in traditional religion and neither were Oliver Fox or Sylvan Muldoon. While I do consider myself a Christian, I myself have pestered God with enough complaints and questions about the state of the world that I'm not sure He/She would consider me a true believer either. This astral world is bigger than religious conviction.

## COMMON GROUND

Another fascinating aspect of astral travel is the similar sensations reported by astral projectors throughout history. Before the advent of mass media and modern communication—before radio, TV, or Google—astral travelers described feeling the same sensations as their souls left their bodies. First there's a bright light, then a tingling sensation throughout the body that is often followed by a loud sound, Then the soul is free. Emanuel Swedenborg wrote of this in his dream journal: "There came over me a very powerful tremor from the head to the feet, accompanied with a booming sound as if many winds had clashed against one another." He then recounts being seated before Christ who told him: "Love me truly and do what thou hast promised." When Swedenborg returned to his body, he was singing the hymn "Jesus Is My Friend, the Very Best One."

Many near-death experiencers and astral travelers believe this tingling sensation and loud sound are linked to our soul leaving the frequency at which the Earth vibrates. Perhaps the hemi-sync program Robert Monroe created to assist astral projection is just one way to help us transcend this sound frequency. If a sonic boom occurs when an object travels faster than the speed of sound, then perhaps these astral travelers are hearing these loud sounds because their souls are traveling faster than sound.

If these ideas intrigue you, consider examining the CIA's unclassified documents on their remote viewing studies, in which they asked intuitives to examine people and locations at a distance with their minds alone. For example, remote reviewer Ingo Swann, working with Russell Targ and Hal Putoff, remote viewed Jupiter and saw rings around the planet in 1973. The Voyager I spacecraft confirmed these rings in 1979, six years after Swann first saw them while remote viewing.

After studying astral travel and reviewing my own personal experiences, I believe it's possible that remote viewing is a form of astral projection achieved during the waking state. The CIA's experiments led them to conclude that all information is "out there." Everything we want to know, see, understand, or experience exists in the astral dimensions. The key is finding an almost magical balance of believing, quieting the mind, taming the ego, and allowing ourselves to slip into a liminal state where time does not exist. And if time doesn't exist, perhaps we can see the future and understand the past by visiting it *now*.

In the next chapter, we'll look at past-life dreams to discover the links that tie us to one another and how all these soul-traveling experiences can help us understand ourselves and our souls' purpose more fully.

## Exercise: Astral Journey

Allow yourself to enter a relaxed state of mind before falling asleep. You can listen to a guided meditation, play relaxing music, or just let the sound of silence wash over you. Close your eyes and stare up into your forehead to activate and awaken your third eye.

Become aware of your aura. Pull your energy into your body and let yourself connect with your physical body on a deep level. Consciously send relaxing energy into all areas of your body, starting at your feet and finishing at your head. Tell each muscle, organ, tissue, and cell to relax and release any stress. Visualize your energy condensing into a ball of light at your solar plexus chakra (right above your navel). See the silver cord connecting your energy to your body.

Imagine yourself floating up and out of your body. See the ball of energy that is you emerging out of your crown chakra (at the top of your head) and visualize yourself rising above your body. Imagine looking down at your body from the ceiling as you continue breathing deeply.

Next, imagine yourself traveling anywhere on the planet you would like to see. Visualize yourself safely soaring through the night sky. See the moon close to you, visualize the trees and roof tops below you as you float, feeling freer than a bird.

Continue this visualization until you fall asleep. The more comfortable you become with "imagining" this form of astral journey, the more easily you'll be able to accomplish this in your soul travels.

# Chapter 9

# PAST-LIFE DREAMS

*We don't sleep merely to live, but to learn to live well.*
Synesius of Cyrene

More and more people are starting to believe in reincarnation thanks to researchers like Jim Tucker, Ian Stevenson, and Carol Bowman. A 2015 study revealed that 25 percent of Christians believe in past lives, and many believe this number is growing. Some theologians speculate that aspects of reincarnation were deliberately removed from the Bible, either during the Second Council of Constantinople or the Council of Nicaea, but a few tidbits remain, like people asking Jesus if he is John the Baptist come again.

Henry David Thoreau, the Transcendentalist writer best known for his book *Walden*, believed in past lives. He had dreams and recollections of past lives. "I lived in Judea 1800 years ago," he claimed. "As far back as I can remember I have unconsciously referred to the experience of a previous state of existence." Robert Louis Stevenson, author of *Treasure Island* and other famous novels, dreamed he was

Jonathon Swift as he lay dying, sensing his emotions and thoughts. Television shows like *Surviving Death* and *The Ghost Inside My Child,* and books like *Return to Life* and *Old Souls* have all presented strong cases for past-life recall. The evidence is clearly growing to support reincarnation.

Past-life regressionists have long reported the healing aspects of recalling a prior life. Individuals have healed phobias, nightmares, allergies, and other ailments after remembering a previous incarnation. There are countless stories of people suffering from claustrophobia until they recall being buried alive or walled up in a prison in a past life. Likewise, there are stories of people who have terrifying fears of water only to have these healed when they recall drowning in a previous incarnation.

## REVISITING PAST LIVES

In "Have We Really Lived Before?" hypnotherapist Michael Pollack writes about how he suffered most of his life from lower back pain. After undergoing a few past-life regression sessions, he claims:

> I discovered that I had lived at least three prior lifetimes in which I had been killed by being knifed or speared in the lower back. After processing and healing the past life experiences, my back began to heal.

Psychiatrist Ian Stevenson devoted his life to studying children's past-life recall. In a paper titled "Birthmarks and Birth Defects Corresponding to Wounds on Deceased Persons," he produced story after story that revealed that birthmarks and other marks on the body often corelate directly with past-life traumas. For example, a boy who had a birthmark on his chest remembered that he was a man named Maha Ram who died of a gunshot wound to the chest in a previous life. When Stevenson confirmed Maha Ram's life and death and compared his autopsy records with the young boy's birthmark, the wound and birthmark were a match.

Carol Bowman, a well-known past-life researcher, writes about her son's past-life memory. When he was a little boy, he suffered from terrible eczema on his wrist and had a deep fear of loud noises like cars backfiring or fireworks. Bowman, who was studying past-life regression, asked her teacher to talk to her son. While sitting on his mom's lap, the boy was gently regressed and recalled a life in which he had been a slave fighting for the Union Army during the Civil War. He was shot in the wrist and taken to a makeshift hospital, bandaged up, and sent back to the battlefield.

The boy talked about how war was not at all like he thought it would be. Although only a preschooler, he described in detail the sound of gun fire and the sight of wagons, horses, and cannon. After this recall session, the eczema on his wrist disappeared. So did his fear of loud noises. Today, as a grown man, he plays the drums and remembers little about his past life. Studies tell us that this is very common. Most past-life memories start to fade by age five or six.

But they still exist in our unconscious. Through the power of dreams, we can start to recall past-life experiences that may be hindering our progress today. In *Children Who Remember Past Lives*, Stephenson wrote: "Some vivid and recurrent dreams may stem from actual memories of previous lives." He says these dreams tend to have a paranormal component to them, and, like visitation dreams, they feel very real. In Guiley's *Dreamwork for the Soul*, she argues:

> [If] a thread links all our lives together, and [if] we have a pattern of karma from this life to the next, then reincarnational dreams show us past lives involving pieces of that karma. These might include fears, phobias, prejudices, behavior patterns and so on that are repeating in the present life.

## PAST-LIFE DREAMS

A listener recently emailed me about a persistent past-life dream memory that she had as a child:

> To this day, I remember "dreaming" about driving a concrete mixer, which sounds extremely odd . . . trust me, I know. The thing that makes this so different is it didn't feel like a dream; I felt like I was actually there. I was in a different body, a man's body. Next thing I know, my toddler self wakes up. I don't remember anything before this.

It is literally the earliest memory I can recall. I don't know why, but this has bothered me for most of my life. Like something about it I just can't put my finger on. Everything about it was so real.

This is a hallmark of a past-life dream. They are incredibly vivid and real. They feel more like memories than dreams and are always accompanied by deep-seated feelings. Many report awakening from a past-life dream recall filled with intense emotions, as if the experience had just happened to them.

Some past-life dreams are lucid, in that you're aware of dreaming while experiencing the past life. Others are focused on you as the observer, as if you were watching a movie scene unfold before you in which you know every character. In the past-life dreams I've experienced, I am both the participant and the observer. There's the "me" in the dream who's experiencing and living through the past-life memory, and then there's the "me" who's alive and well in the present watching the memory unfold in the dream.

I've had several past-life dreams. I remember one of them very clearly because it felt so real and because it occurred on Thanksgiving morning. At the time, I had two daughters, one eighteen months old and one just four weeks old. In the dream, I was seated at the kitchen table feeding the youngest, who was sitting up in a highchair. The fact that she was already sitting up and talking at just four weeks didn't seem to surprise the dreaming "me" at all.

Then the younger child asked me if I wanted to know why she and her sister had chosen me to be their mother. When I said yes, she took my hand and said: "I'll show you."

Suddenly I was standing in a one-room schoolhouse. I knew instinctively that the young woman teaching the small group of children was me in a prior life. I watched as two little girls came in holding hands. They both looked tired, disheveled, and in great need of a bath. I told the class to read for a while and headed to the back of the room. I scooped the little girls into a hug and motioned them over to a wash basin. As I began helping them wash their faces, I recognized the girls as my daughters. When I wiped the dirt off their faces, I noticed a large bruise on the older girl's face.

I said, "Is he at it again?"

She nodded, but said nothing.

In the next instant, I was standing outside a farmhouse watching as the two little girls were led out of the house. In the dream, I knew my girls had arrived at this farmhouse as orphans and were now being moved again. The girls also knew they were being removed from the home and that they were being separated. Both were crying and clinging to each other. I felt every emotion of the schoolteacher in that moment—guilt, remorse, helplessness, and fear that I had done the wrong thing.

Then my youngest daughter turned to me and said: "We were orphans before we came here. Even though it was bad here, we didn't want to be separated. We wanted to be sisters for real this time, so we chose you because we knew you'd love us forever, and we'd be safe." Then she laughed and added: "We wanted to be twins, but you wouldn't let us," In the next moment, we were back in our kitchen.

I woke back in my bed and went over and over the dream for a long time. Even though it was Thanksgiving morning and I had several people coming to the house in a few short hours, I couldn't move from my bed. So many details of this dream made sense to me. I was a teacher in this life too. I was also terrified of having twins. My mother is a twin and I knew that, since it skipped a generation genetically, there was a good chance I would have twins. My cousin and my sister both have twins. When I was trying to conceive my first child, I asked God to please gift me with one child at a time.

As I mentioned in chapter 6, I believe we choose our parents. This dream showed me that my girls had chosen me as their mom, not only so they could be sisters "for real" this time, but also to help me overcome the immense guilt I carried from that past life. In the dream, I was aware of the schoolteacher's emotions and knew she'd gone to her death wondering what happened to those precious little girls. Reincarnation occurs to help us work through these feelings of guilt and remorse, through fears and dashed hopes. We are born again into each life with an elaborate soul plan detailing the opportunities we have within us to undo years of karma and challenges that have held our souls back. Past-life studies have shown that simply recalling these prior incarnations can help us heal that karma.

# HEALING KARMA

Karma is the accumulation of your soul's actions since the time of its creation to the present. All the good you've done in all your lifetimes builds up "good" karma. Conversely, all the good you haven't done—from missed chances to help someone or missed opportunities to live up to your highest potential, to negative acts like lying, cheating, or stealing—create "bad" karma. Throughout the ages, spiritual teachers have taught that we return lifetime after lifetime in an effort to heal the bad karma and build more good karma.

I'm not sure it's as simple as that, however. Our soul's plan is much more complex than we can comprehend. If you cheated on your spouse in your last life, it doesn't mean you came back in this life simply to experience adultery from the other perspective. Karma is, however, a real aspect of our soul's development. We are given many opportunities to heal our karma through spiritual awakenings, therapy, self-care, and dream work.

If you have a recurring pattern in your life that shows up again and again, this can be an indication of a karmic pattern that needs to be healed. Take some time to review your life and look at the missing aspects. Are you constantly worried about money? Looking for love? Feeling like a victim? Or dealing with health issues? These repeating patterns are trying to tell you something. They're like red flags warning you to pay attention and telling you that this is what you're here to work on.

One client who came to me for Reiki was working on a lot of personal healing and wanted to spend an hour each week on my table focused on shifting her energy. The second time she came to see me, I was working on her heart chakra with my eyes closed. Suddenly, I no longer felt that I was in my cozy little office with the whir of the rose quartz fountain lulling us into a peaceful state. Instead, I saw myself in a brothel above a saloon. A woman with dark brown hair was lying across the bed, waiting for her man. I sat down next to her and asked her to tell me what was wrong. She held my hands and told me that, for years, a man visited her every time he came through town. Each time, he promised he'd leave his wife and run off with her. But after each visit, he left with another excuse. My client shifted on the table and, instantly, I was back in the room. The vivid scene shook me, and I ended the session shortly thereafter.

When I recounted what I'd seen in this vision to my client, she clapped a hand over her mouth and said: "That's so weird! When I was lying on the table, I kept thinking of a dream I had last week." In the dream, she saw herself as a young woman in her mid-thirties with brown hair who was languishing in a shabby room above a bar waiting for a man who would never rescue her. When she asked how that could be, I told her that it was most likely a past-life memory pattern that she was repeating right now, and that this was her soul's way of trying to heal this pattern once and for all. She started to cry and told me that she was dating her boss, who had been separated from his wife for five years.

I told her to write down as much of the dream as she could remember and to maintain an attitude of openness to more dreams. When she returned the next week, she reported having another dream in which she was married to the man she was currently dating, but that he had a mistress whom he truly loved. She said that the feeling in this dream was exactly the same as in the brothel dream. She felt as if she were wasting her life waiting for the man to love her. And in both dreams the man's right thumb was broken and twisted. Her boyfriend's thumb was also broken and twisted from an old injury.

This woman had lived two different lifetimes waiting for a man to return her affection. In one, she was the devoted wife; in the other, she was the mistress. Neither had worked out. She was faced with the same scenario in this life. Except this time, she was a highly educated woman of the 21st century who had choices and options. It took her another four months, but eventually she left her married boyfriend. The dreams stopped and, within a year, she moved and met her future husband, who loves her just as much as she loves him.

A close member of my family had a recurring dream that always made her question past lives. Shortly after I was born, she began having recurrent dreams that I was drowning and she was trying (and failing) to rescue me. We wondered if this had indeed happened in a past life, but since I don't have a fear of water or drowning, we decided this was unlikely and it was probably a subconscious dream.

As I grew up, the dreams stopped until she gave birth to her first child. Then she began to dream that her daughter was drowning and, again, she kept failing to save the baby. When she gave birth to her son, the dreams switched, and now it was her son who was drowning. But this time, she saved him and the dreams stopped. Years later, she had a reading with an intuitive who told her that, in a past life, her child had died in a drowning accident and that these dreams were probably her way of working through the karmic pain of guilt, loss, and remorse.

My sister had nightmares as a child that she could never fully recall. They were so traumatic that she was often found sleep-walking. Once she entered elementary school, the dreams stopped. But when she was in high school, she tried a past-life meditation technique that brought back the memory of her childhood nightmare. She was a little girl sweeping an elaborate foyer of a mansion. As she swept the floor, she began dancing with the broom, causing a crystal vase to crash and break. The cruel owner of the home forced the little girl's mother, who worked there as a kitchen maid, to beat her own daughter as punishment. She felt that by simply remembering this experience, she was sending healing, acknowledgment, and recognition to this frightened little girl down the generational lines of karma.

One friend told me that she had a life-changing past-life dream that helped her heal a relationship with her sister-in-law. For some reason, her sister-in-law had hated her from day one. There was no rhyme or reason to it; she just didn't like her. She tried everything to get on the woman's good side, but it was as if she hated her just because she loved her brother. Four years into her marriage, my friend was dreading the upcoming holiday season because she knew her sister-in-law would attack her with biting and rude remarks about her appearance, her home, and her cooking. Her husband felt caught between the two women he loved so much.

A few nights before the sister-in-law's arrival, my friend fell asleep after journaling about her worries over this relationship. She dreamed that she was walking through cobblestone streets carrying a baby and a basket of vegetables.

> The scenery made me feel that I was back in the 1500s. I was wearing a long, worn cotton cream-colored dress. I knew the baby wasn't mine, but I loved her as though she were. I was happy in this moment. I had "my" baby in my arms, the sun was shining, and I knew the man I loved was returning soon from battle.
>
> I walked up old stone stairs into the back of a castle, where an older woman told me the mistress of the house was waiting for me in her rooms. When I walked in, still holding the precious baby, I saw that the woman was my sister-in-law from this lifetime. The man I loved was standing by her side. It was my husband, but in this lifetime, he was my sister-in-law's husband.
>
> I knew instantly that we loved each other and had been having an affair for years. I also knew I was the baby's nursemaid, and that this baby and I were very attached. My sister-in-law crudely snatched the baby out of my arms and ordered me to leave the castle. The baby started to cry and reached for me. I felt the pain of our loss

and separation in every cell of my body. I fell to my knees and begged her to change her mind. But she was adamant. Her husband—my husband now—just looked at me meekly as I turned to leave.

After this dream, my friend said that everything changed for her. She and her husband entered therapy, where she was able to get him to see that he needed to stand up for his wife. And the visit with her sister-in-law went smoothly. "I don't know if this was a magical effect of the dream," she said, "or if I had just softened a bit since I now understood why she disliked me on an unconscious level." But the best thing that came out of this dream was that, soon after, my friend delivered a beautiful baby girl. "I realized that I finally had it all—the man I loved, our baby, and, slowly but surely, a better relationship with my sister-in-law."

Karma we carry over from other lifetimes can't necessarily be healed in just one past-life dream. But these dream experiences can act as signposts that help us wake up to what our subconscious is trying to show us. These dreams can help us navigate through difficult relationships or repressed fears and begin the healing journey of understanding, inner peace, and self-love.

## ANNOUNCING DREAMS

Ian Stevenson coined the term "announcing dreams" to describe dreams in which a soul announces it is soon to be born. He includes many of these dream stories in his books, like the dream U Po Min's aunt had shortly before her niece gave birth. In the dream, U Po Min's grandmother said she was returning to her grandchild as a daughter. The grandmother said in the dream: "If you don't believe me, I'll be born with the feet first. You will also see that the toes will be joined to the foot." The baby girl was born breech with two toes of her right foot joined together.

In another story, as a man named Vincent lay dying, he told his niece that he would be born again as her child. He said she'd recognize him because he'd have the same two scars he carried then—one on his nose and the other on his back. He added that he hoped this reincarnated version of himself wouldn't have to suffer with stuttering as he had in this lifetime. Eighteen months after his death, the niece gave birth to a boy who had two marks on his body in the exact places Vincent had said they'd appear—on his nose and back. The child suffered with a strong stutter until he was nine. He also recognized several friends of Vincent's and shared his fascination with engines.

I experienced my own announcing dream just a few years ago. When my friend Jeff died, I often had dreams about him in which we simply visited and caught up. It was lovely to be able to connect with him in this dream state, but years later, the dreams faded and eventually stopped. One afternoon, I meditated with the express intent of reaching Jeff. I felt nothing. It was as if he were no longer on the other side. That night, I had a dream that I was walking with him through a beautiful garden and he told me that he was getting ready to incarnate again to his youngest brother. I called another friend and asked him if

Jeff's younger brother was expecting a child. He said no, and warned me that, sometimes, a dream is just a dream.

Three months later, our mutual friend called to say that Jeff's little brother just announced that his wife was pregnant. They had a little boy, whom they decided to name Jeffrey.

Often, announcing dreams are a bit more subtle than this. One night, I had a fairly mundane dream about visiting a park with my husband and our two daughters. As we pushed them in their swings, I suddenly noticed a third little girl sitting in the last swing waiting to be pushed. When I awoke, I heard the name "Chloe" ringing out through the bedroom. When I suggested to my husband that, if we ever had another daughter, we name her Chloe, he said, "I love that name!" I was surprised, because it had taken us months to agree on the names for our first two daughters.

When I became pregnant again, I had a recurring dream throughout the pregnancy that my daughter would be born at 11:27 PM. At least once a month, I dreamed that, when I delivered Chloe, I looked at a digital clock that read 11:27. I thought it was such a small detail to dream over and over. As I'm sure you can guess by now, Chloe was born at exactly 11:27 PM.


## CONFRONTING FEARS

The unspoken fears that you're afraid to voice even to yourself are the challenges you most need to face in your life. This is often done most gently through dreams. One of my biggest fears was "coming out" of the psychic closet.

I was terrified of what my friends would say and how my co-workers would judge me. At the time, I was a member of a mothers' prayer group and a rosary group. Would they kick me out when they learned that I was doing "weird" readings?

I fell asleep one hot July evening ruminating on all of this and had an incredibly vivid dream. I was a woman in my mid-forties dressed in a beautiful, sapphire silk gown. I was hosting a salon in my upstairs apartment overlooking the streets of Paris. I knew I made my living doing readings, and I understood how dangerous this work was. Yet, somehow, my attitude as I prepared the room with candles and crystals was one of careless frivolity. My maid kept following me from room to room as I gathered up supplies. She was frantically telling me that what I was doing was too dangerous, and I needed to stop. I smiled condescendingly and told her that I was reading for both sides, so neither the revolutionaries or the nobles could touch me.

Suddenly, there was a loud banging on the door. Before my maid could answer it, several men barged through and arrested me. In the dream, I called out to my maid: "This is the work of Count Delacroix."

I awoke with a start and lay in bed going over and over the dream. It seemed more like a memory than a dream. I felt the emotions of the woman, her remorse at taking her gifts so lightly and flaunting her abilities to anyone who would pay her. I knew this man, Delacroix, had somehow crossed her. When I opened my journal to record the dream, I was shocked when I wrote the date: July 14—Bastille

Day. Had I been one of the nameless, faceless victims guillotined with so many others during the French Revolution? Was this death the primary reason I was so afraid to "come out" of the psychic closet? I lit a candle that day and kept it lit every day until it burned down. Each morning, I said a prayer for this woman's life as I lit the candle and asked that her fears (my fears?) be healed and released.

Soon after this experience, my boss asked me to do a reading for her. I was terrified to comply. What if nothing came through? What if I got everything wrong? How would this effect my job? Luckily, the reading went very well. When I turned up at her office to go over my fall schedule, I was stunned when she handed me a blank piece of paper.

"What is this?" I asked. "Am I fired?"

She smiled and said: "No. I am giving you wings, Samantha. You have a gift. A gift from God that must be shared with the world. Go and do God's work. This job will be here if you need it. But you must do this work." And that's how I started doing readings full time. I don't think I would have received the push I needed if I hadn't had this past-life dream. It enabled me to recognize and release my fears over being a "weird intuitive."

A listener to my podcast shared a powerful past-life dream that helped him release an unspoken fear. He was a veteran who'd served in Iraq and Afghanistan. He was smart and good-looking, but found himself unable to commit to a relationship. When he had retired from the Marines, he was battling PTSD, which led him to practice meditation. In an email, he wrote:

I'm not sure if it was the meditation or just right timing, but after about a year of meditating every day, I had a series of dreams that lasted for months. In each dream, I was a soldier in a different time period. I'm not great at history so I can't be sure as to dates. I just know that in each of these dreams I was fighting a war. In one dream, I had long, braided hair and felt that I was like a Viking or something. In another, I did recognize a WWI uniform. I looked it up on the internet, and I think I was a German officer. Anyway, in every dream, I died in battle and left a widow at home grieving for me.

In the last dream I had, I was walking through a battlefield with a person who was like my guide or maybe an angel. I don't know. But this guy was walking with me as we made our way through all these bodies on the ground. He said: "You've fought bravely my son. But the hardest battle to fight is the one with your heart. It's time to open your heart to love and leave the battlefield to its own grave."

When I woke up, I was crying. I'm not a guy who cries, but this intense emotion of grief just came over me. It stayed with me all day. What the heck are these dreams about?

I emailed back and told him that it seemed as if these dreams were past-life memories calling out through time to be healed and released. I recommended that he choose a crystal-like black kyanite, nuumite, snowflake obsidian, or apatite to hold as he works to release any unconscious memories from these past lives. I told him to create a mantra that he could repeat each day—something like: "I am loved, loving, and open to love."

I didn't hear back from him for several years. Then just last month, he emailed to say that he had done the work to release his past-life memories and realized that he'd been terrified of committing to someone in this life.

> Somehow in my head, I think I subconsciously tied loving someone to me dying. But once I worked on letting that go, I released all that and met my wife. We have a daughter now and are expecting our second child this fall.

When we maintain an openness to these kinds of dreams, we can experience not only emotional healing, but even physical healing.

A friend of mine had been trying for years to get pregnant with little success. She and her husband finally decided to try IVF. When that didn't succeed, she began praying fervently for any help or insight into her fertility issues. In the following weeks, she had two vivid past-life dreams. In one, she saw herself as a concubine to a cruel emperor. Each time she got pregnant and delivered a child, the baby was taken from her. In another, she saw herself dying in childbirth. As she worked to heal these fears rooted in her past-life memories, her marriage ended. The following year, she met her current husband and conceived a child naturally, without the help of IVF or hormones. Her sweet baby is now almost ten years old.

The soul is always seeking to heal trauma and resolve fears. Past-life recall is one way for the soul to do this. You can go to a trained regressionist or you can try regressing yourself. I think it's always a good idea to set an intention for the regression—something like: "It is my intention to review the past life that is blocking my progress now." Or: "It is my intention to view the past life that needs to be healed now." And you can also heal old traumas from past lives through dreams.

Recalling our past lives, whether through past-life regression or dreams, helps us recognize patterns in our present lives, understand the reasons behind painful events, and obtain a deeper appreciation of karma. Most importantly, it helps us to truly know and love ourselves. As you work to remember your dreams in tandem with maintaining an open mind as to what these dreams reveal to you, you'll greatly increase your chances of having a past-life dream.

## Exercise: Past-Life Dream Recall

Lie in bed and allow yourself to get into a relaxed state of mind. Listen to some relaxing music, shamanic drumming, or binaural beats. With your eyes closed, stare up into your forehead to activate and awaken your third eye. Count backward from 100 to 1. With each decade you count down, envision yourself descending a staircase. Repeat to yourself: "I will dream about my past life."

When you get to the last stair, visualize a door that opens into your childhood bedroom. Take some time walking through this memory. See the color on the walls. Feel the fabric of your comforter. Visualize yourself sitting on the bed. As this memory from your past returns to you, feel yourself sinking farther and farther back in time.

Soon you feel pulled to walk through your bedroom door. As you open this door, see yourself walking into one of your earliest, happy memories. It could be a birthday party or a trip to Disney World. Allow yourself to engage all your senses as you recall and relive this happy event. As you relax into this old memory, you suddenly notice another door. As you walk toward it, tell yourself that it will open to a vision of your past life.

When you walk through this door, look down at your feet. Are you barefooted or wearing shoes? What do the shoes look like? Are you walking on grass? On a paved road? Across a hardwood floor? Take some time to look around and walk through this memory. Are there people with you? If so, do you recognize them? Mentally tell yourself to walk to the happiest memory from this lifetime.

See yourself enjoying this happy memory as you take note of the people with you and any emotions you're feeling. When you're ready, ask yourself to move to a memory that holds a challenge you're still confronting in this lifetime. Be sure to breathe deeply and remind yourself that this is just a memory. Continue with these visualizations until you fall asleep, trusting that your soul will travel to a past-life dream memory.

# Chapter 10

# GUIDES AND ANGELS

*Whoever travels without a guide needs two hundred years for a two day journey.*

Rumi

It's often said that we are born alone, and we die alone. I completely disagree with this sentiment. I believe that we arrive on Earth surrounded by a team of helpers called spirit guides and guardian angels. And when we die, this same team helps us to cross over to the other side, where we're greeted by loved ones who've gone before us.

Earth is a school, however. And just as our teachers in school can't follow us around wherever we go, shouting out the answers to tests and reminding us to do our homework, our guides and angels can't give us all the answers. What they can do is offer help throughout our journey. And this help will often appear in our dreams when we're soul traveling as they check in with us, bringing an energy of hope or offering suggestions to help us on our way.

# SPIRIT GUIDES

Spirit guides are highly evolved souls who have lived before. As we prepare to come to Earth, our guides help us create a blueprint, a map, for our soul's journey in this lifetime. Every one of us has at least one spirit guide who is with us from our first breath to our last. Their purpose is to help keep us on our path, to help us follow the blueprint we laid out for ourselves before birth.

In addition to our main guide, we work with several other guides who join our team as we progress through life. We have teacher guides who come into our lives when we start school. When we deal with an illness, healer guides come in to help us. Some guides join the team to help us with romance or careers, or to help us develop our talents and gifts. If we choose to become parents, parenting guides join the team. If we have to help a parent, spouse, or partner through their last chapter on Earth, caretaker guides appear to show us the way.

We also have guides I call our "cheerleaders." These are often comedians, actors, jesters, or entertainers who have a hugely uplifting energy. Their sole job is to be the wind beneath our wings, to lift us up and help us remember to laugh when times get tough.

We also have protector guides whose job is to guard and protect our energy. But they cannot protect us from learning our lessons. Let's say that you met someone in your twenties to whom you were instantly drawn. It felt like perfect kismet. This is often a sign that you have karma to balance with this person. The person may have hurt you in a past life and it may be your karma in this life simply to be with this person and engage the hurt again. But this time, your soul wants to learn how to move past this hurt.

Can your guides save you from this person hurting you? No. It's your karma, your choice, your path. But they can protect you by putting the right people in your path to help you navigate your way through setting boundaries and healing this karma once and for all. Maybe, as you're nursing the heartache, your guides will help you meet a great new friend, or someone may recommend a wonderful therapist, or you may happen upon a book that helps you heal. These are all ways in which your guides will help you.

Many religions and cultures have long believed in spirit guides. The ancient Greeks believed in a guardian *daemon,* an elevated being who assists you in your decisions—not to be confused with the Christian demon. Socrates often wrote about his daemon, referring to him as a non-local voice or an inner nudge that didn't tell him what to do, but rather guided him to seek the best path. Shamans go into meditation to achieve an altered state of consciousness in order to connect with their guides. Carl Jung wrote about encountering his guide, a being he called Philemon.

Spirit guides, like our departed loved ones in heaven, can connect with us in our waking life most easily through signs and synchronicity. Since metal is a conductor of energy, coins have long been seen as a sign from the other side, hence the phrase "pennies from heaven." Guides often use music to link to us as well. Pay attention to songs on the radio or lyrics that randomly pop into your mind. Guides may also place animals in your path to bring a message of peace or comfort. If, for example, you're ruminating on a past issue that's blocking your progress, you may see a grasshopper. Grasshoppers can only jump forward, not back, or left, or right. Seeing one in your daily life can be a sign that it's time to move forward. Cardinals are universally recognized as a hello from heaven. Butterflies are seen to symbolize transformation, not death, as the caterpillar "dies" to be reborn as a butterfly.

However, not every butterfly or cardinal you see is a sign from above. True signs will appear to you in either an unusual way or with perfect timing. When my friend was dealing with a negative work situation, she applied for a new job. When she got an offer, she couldn't decide what to do. Should she keep the familiar job or take a risk on this new offer? As she sat in her living room looking out the window praying to God, she asked for a sign to tell her if she should stay or go. Suddenly, a grasshopper appeared on her window ledge and stayed there for several moments— long enough for her to take a quick photo. She took this as a sign that it was time to move forward and accepted the new position, which has made her much happier.

One of the best ways to connect with your spirit guides is through your dreams. Most of us have so much doubt buried deep within the layers of our aura that contact with these elevated beings is difficult during our waking life. But when we sleep and our egoic, conscious minds rest, we're able to dissolve these walls and connect with our helpers.

When I began on my spiritual path, I wanted to know who my main guide was. I meditated almost every day for six months with the specific intent of contacting my guide.

The meditations felt lovely. I often saw beautiful colors or received feelings of peace and universal love, but it took six months of consistent effort before I saw my guide. Even then, it was just a brief flash of a Native American figure.

As my spiritual learning progressed, I began teaching English by day and doing practice readings in the evening. I was struggling inside to determine my future path. Should I continue teaching and rely on the safety of a "normal" job, complete with healthcare and benefits? Or should I take a leap of faith and begin doing readings full time? I had a dream in which I was sitting on the swing in my backyard looking up at the Full Moon when I saw my guide walking across the lawn toward me. He held a large feather in his hand. I sat in awe and watched as he held my hands and anointed each palm with the feather saying: "It is time."

I knew he meant it was time for me to take a leap of faith and leave my safe job. Still, I felt nervous and scared about what this enormous change would mean for me. As a Catholic, I also worried about opening myself up to the other side. What if I encountered something negative? After journaling all my fears, I dreamed that my guide was with me in a forest. I was standing in the middle of a clearing as he and several of his family members gathered around me in a circle. They were throwing threads over and under me, weaving a giant dream catcher around my energy. When the beautiful, intricate design was completed, my guide said: "I will always protect and guide you."

Each connection with my guide left me feeling safe, but also humbled. He's truly a man of wisdom, faith, and silent strength. I wanted to know his name, so I asked him in a meditation and heard: "Chippewa." I Googled the name and learned that it's not his actual name, but rather the name of an Algonquian-speaking people also known as the Ojibwe. They are best known for storytelling—and for making dream catchers.

If you fall asleep ruminating on a problem or concern, your guides can use the dream time to help you see this issue from a different perspective. When I was having an issue with a coworker, I felt I was between a rock and a hard place. This woman loved to argue with everyone. I often found myself embroiled in heated debates with her over trivial matters. When we were tasked with coteaching, it became disastrous. We had completely different teaching styles. I fell asleep wondering how the students and I would survive the next sixteen weeks dealing with her hard-nosed approach.

Then I dreamed that she and I were having a tug of war over a huge mud puddle. I felt my guide standing next to me and clearly heard him say: "Let go." As I let go of the rope, I watched as my co-worker fell into the mud puddle. The next day at school, I followed his advice. I let go of the fighting. I surrendered to her way of teaching. Soon the students fought back against the ridiculous workload, and, by the end of the month, I had a new (and much kinder) coteacher.

Guides will often appear in our dreams to remind us to stay strong and focused on our path. When I was learning how to enhance my intuition, I was resisting the meditation work each teacher recommended. Wherever I went, I kept hearing: "Meditate, meditate, meditate." I didn't want to meditate. I didn't have the time or the interest to meditate. Then one night, I had a dream that really brought home a message I'd been receiving: "Girl, you gotta work."

In the dream, I saw the Tree of Life. It resembled the one from the Animal Kingdom at Disney World, but was much larger—easily over 200 feet high. The roots were massive. I noticed a huge, ornately carved, wooden door nestled in the center of the tree's trunk. As I started toward the door, a short, kind, older man appeared and asked: "Do you want to see the secret back door?" I said I did.

As we walked, he said that this secret door was a short cut to what I was looking for. I remember feeling so excited and thinking: "I knew it! I knew there was a way around all the hard work of meditating each day." We walked around to the side of the massive tree, where he showed me a hidden door that was covered with leaves. As I walked closer to move the leaves aside, he stopped me and said: "No. If you think there's a short cut to the Tree of Life, then you aren't ready."

Wow. Message received. And so I began the process of meditating every day. Well, almost every day. I learned that, like everything I resist in life, once I made it a habit, meditating became easier. It was the work I needed to do to find my way to the front door of the Tree of Life. I haven't encountered this tree again in a dream, but I hope that, if I do, I will have the courage to say: "Nope, I don't want the secret back door. I'm doing the work to prepare for the big front door."

# THE HIGHER SELF

Your spiritual team of guides and helpers includes your higher self—a part of you that always remains on the other side. This is the aspect of your soul that remembers all your lifetimes. It is aware of your soul's blueprint and works with your team of helpers to keep you on your path. Many have connected with their higher selves through meditation and dreams. The co-host of the *Psychic Teachers* podcast, Deb Bowen, shared her mystical dream experience of meeting with her higher self:

> In the dream, I am staring into an Isis-point quartz and the world turns gray. I feel as if I am diving deeply into the crystal. I land on my feet and begin walking through fog thick as smoke. Fog swirls around me as I walk, my feet making no sound as I seem to glide forward. There is no sound, nothing to touch, nothing to see except the fog.
>
> Slowly, the fog begins to clear, and I can hear my feet meeting stone with each step. A ray of sunlight beams down in front of me, and I find myself standing at one end of a stone balcony. The balcony is enclosed in carved Assyrian balustrades of the same stone.
>
> Beyond the balcony, a cerulean sea surrounds me, and in the distance, I see ships sailing and dinghies rowing toward a distant shore overshadowed by cliffs. Gleaming white houses, stacked

like layers on a wedding cake, climb the cliffs above the water.

Suddenly, my attention is drawn back to the balcony in front of me. A woman stands at the other end, facing me, her back to the sea. She is very tall and dark, with long rippling black hair. She is wearing a white gown, softly draping around her. Her eyes—her eyes are magical. They are black, black, black, and huge. Staring at me softly. I know I've known her for a thousand lifetimes. I know I've known her beyond the Earth plane. She is speaking to me without speaking.

"I have been with you forever and shall always be. I know you better than you will ever know yourself. Nothing has ever been, nor can ever be, hidden between us. I am not your Guide. I am You. I am that part of you that lives forever on a higher plane. To me you will return, to learn and to grow and to be born again and again and again."

She faded away and then the scene before me fades away and I wake up.

I've yet to encounter my own higher self in a dream or a meditation. I feel confident, however, that, if I did, she wouldn't be as eloquent as Deb's was. She'd probably give me an eye roll before saying: "Did you even read your soul's blueprint?" I have, however, had wonderful dream experiences with the angelic realm.

# GUARDIAN ANGELS

Angels are beings who have never lived as humans—with some exceptions. It's said, for instance, that the prophet Enoch was taken up to heaven and became the angel Metatron.

Angels are messengers of God. The word "angel" in fact comes from the Greek word *angelos*, which means "messenger." The Hebrew word for angel is *malakh*, which also means "messenger." The Persian word for angel is *angaros*, which means "courier." There are hundreds of examples of angels at work through the centuries. They are mentioned in all major religions—over 300 times in the Bible alone. In the Old Testament, Uriel warns Noah of the flood and God tells Moses: "I am sending my angel to go before you and guard you on your way and lead you to the place I have made ready for you" (Ex 23:20–21). Archangel Michael fought with the devil over Moses' body and helped Joshua and his people at Jericho. Lot talked to two angels and an angel spoke to Abraham in a dream.

It's an angel who stays Abraham's hand when he's about to sacrifice his son. It was an angel who gave Gideon the courage to free his people. Balaam is said to have met his guardian angel when he was traveling to the princes of Moab to curse the nation of Israel. Elijah met an angel who helped nurse him back to health by providing food and water. Isaiah saw the Seraphim, celestial beings who are traditionally placed in the highest rank in Christian angelology. The prophet Daniel was sealed in a cave with lions. When the king returned for him the next day, he said that angels had kept him safe from the beasts. He also said the

Archangel Gabriel had appeared to him and told him that the Messiah was coming.

In the New Testament, Gabriel appeared to Zachariah to tell him that his wife would soon be pregnant with John the Baptist. Later, he appeared to Mary and told her she would give birth to Jesus. He also appeared to Joseph to assure him that Mary was in fact pregnant with the son of God. Angels appeared at Jesus' birth and again to warn Mary and Joseph to flee to Egypt. Angels helped Jesus after the devil tempted him on the mount and again when he was in Gethsemane. Angels were at the tomb when Jesus rose.

Angels helped Peter escape from jail and appeared before Cornelius and told him to go see Peter so he could be baptized. In his epistles, Paul mentions angels many times, speaking of a hierarchy of angelic beings. And angels are mentioned numerous times in the Book of Revelations.

Angels also appear in other religions and cultures. The Hindus write about *avatars*; Buddhists speak of *devas* and *bodhisattvas*. The ancient Greeks wrote about *daemons*, and many different tribal cultures teach that we all have guardian spirits. The Archangel Gabriel helped Mohammed write the Koran, and angels told Joan of Arc how to defeat France. Catholics believe that everyone has a guardian angel and ancient Jewish tradition taught that everyone had 11,000 angels.

I've always believed in angels and have felt their presence around me many times in my life. Maybe it's because I was raised a Catholic, but I always feel unworthy when I sense the angelic realm, which is why connecting with my spirit guides is much easier for me. Yet, angels still make their presence known to me. When I was dating my former husband, Mike, I had a hard time dealing with his career as a police officer. I couldn't imagine spending a lifetime with someone who willingly put his life on the line every day. How would I ever sleep? As a reformed worrier, I knew this would be hard for me.

Then Mike shared with me a dream he had when he was a child. When he was ten, he realized he wanted to be a police officer when he grew up. He even announced it to his family one night at the dinner table. That evening, he awoke while still in a dream. He was lying in his bed, but knew he was still dreaming. He saw the Archangel Michael standing at the foot of his bed holding a sword made of blue light. He said: "Thank you for your decision. It is the right one. Henceforth, I will always protect you."

Mike said he never forgot that dream and often feels the archangel's protective energy around him. Years later, when he was promoted, we got him an Archangel Michael necklace as a celebratory gift. He wore it to work every day tucked under his bullet-proof vest. The night he was shot in the line of duty, a nurse approached and handed me his wedding band and the necklace. Both were covered in his dried blood. I was so angry and scared in that moment that I raged at Archangel Michael in my head: "You were supposed to protect him!"

Then a nurse walked in who described the experience she had in the operating room as they fought to keep Mike alive.

I haven't prayed in a long time. I used to have this wonderful connection to Archangel Michael, but I lost it a long time ago. I used to think of myself as a healer not a nurse. Anyway, suddenly I got this icy cold feeling all over my body. I heard a male voice say: "Touch him on his forehead." I looked around, but no one else had heard that voice. So I did it. I touched him on his forehead and the machine beeped. The doctors yelled: 'We've got a pulse!' I don't know what that voice was, but something miraculous happened in there. I think Archangel Michael healed him. I'm going to church this weekend. That's all I know. Can you please tell the family this story?

Then I thought about the other circumstances that had conspired to help Mike survive—the gun jamming, the paramedics receiving a prank call, the thoracic surgeon being on duty, the supply of the correct blood type. All of this made me realize that some things in life may be destined to occur, but our guides and angels are always there to protect us. Maybe it was Mike's destiny to get shot that night. I don't know. But I do know that Archangel Michael kept his promise.

## CONNECTING WITH YOUR ANGELS

In order to have dream connections with our guardian angels, we have to establish a relationship with them in our daily lives. There's an old story about a woman who arrived in heaven and met an angel who gave her a tour of where the angels lived. As he walked her through the various rooms, she saw that they were crowded with angels. "This is the room where we receive healing requests," the angel told her as they observed countless angels working to send out healing energy. "And this is the room where we receive prayers for the newly deceased." Again, the room was filled with hard-working angels. Finally, they came to a room that was empty save for one lone angel. "What happens in this room?" the woman asked. The angel said sadly: "This is the room where we receive prayers of gratitude for the work we do."

How many times have you prayed for something, received it, and then forgotten to say thank you or even acknowledge that the prayer was fulfilled? But when you connect with your guardian angels through gratitude, prayer, and meditation, you reap huge benefits in your life. And, as with your spirit guides, these connections can be most vivid in the dream state.

Rosemary Ellen Guiley, who wrote many wonderful books on dreams and angels, describes several dream encounters she had with her guardian angel in *Dreamwork for the Soul*. Guiley calls her angel Silver Lady, because she always appears dressed in flowing, luminescent silver robes. Her angel often took her on travels through the spirit world, acting almost as a tour guide for the other side. "These were always big dreams," Guiley recalls, "involving out-of-body travel to other realms, communication by telepathy, and much spiritual instruction, although I could never put words to it or remember it when I awakened." One morning, Guiley awoke to see her angel standing by her bed.

> A strong current of energy was streaming out of her hands and into my heart and third-eye chakras. It was rather like being downloaded through a cosmic modem. When I was pumped full, the connection was broken and Silver Lady disappeared. Later, I felt I had been infused with an alchemical blueprint that would unfold itself throughout the course of my life.

This inability to remember important information from a dream encounter with an angel or spirit guide is common.

I had a dream recently in which I was sitting at a conference table with two of my guides. I was complaining that I wasn't remembering these dreams and all the important information I received in my waking life. In the dream, I said: "Why go to all the trouble of appearing in my dream to impart sacred, important stuff if I can't remember it in its entirety upon waking? That makes no sense." One of my guides reached across the table for my hands and said: "Your soul remembers. That is all that matters."

Emanuel Swedenborg also writes in his journals about forgetting his dreams.

> All that I dreamt was in answer to my thoughts, yet in such a manner that I cannot describe the least particular, for all of it was heavenly. At the

time it was clear to me, but after it I cannot express anything.

Many near-death experiencers also recount being on the other side and receiving all the answers to life's mysteries, but forgetting everything upon returning to Earth. I hope my spirit guide is right. Our souls remember and that is enough. Perhaps these "forgotten" experiences are retained in our unconscious and will rise to the surface when our waking selves are ready to accept, assimilate, and fully comprehend these mystical concepts.

We often have dreams of our angels and guides that don't seem to make sense at the time. When I was taking my first baby steps into the world of intuition, I had just earned my Reiki I degree. I started to learn about crystals and joined an intuitive development group. One evening, I had a dream that I was walking through an empty house. When I climbed the staircase to the upper floors, a woman in a full nun's habit greeted me in the hallway flanked by two angels. She smiled and said her name. I couldn't comprehend it—something I still don't understand. She smiled again and said: "You can just call me Sister Veronica." I nodded and tried to remember her face. She had dark hair peeking out from under her wimple and rich, brown eyes matched by a kind smile that put me at ease. She said: "Are you willing to work for God and Jesus?" I quickly said I was and she nodded and said: "Very well. You will start in six weeks."

I awoke with so much excitement. I marked the calendar for six weeks in the future. Nothing happened that week. But the following week at my intuitive development class, I brought through someone's guide with strong validations and received information from another classmate's mom and brother on the other side. Suddenly, students from the class began calling me for readings. I couldn't connect the dots at the time, but it marked the beginning of my journey into working with guides, angels, and offering readings.

I had another wonderful encounter with the angelic realm through dreams the night before my mastectomy surgery. I was terrified and had barely been sleeping. But this night, when I finally dosed for a bit, I had a dream that I was walking next to the ocean with a woman. She had long brown hair and was wearing a dolphin necklace. She didn't have wings, but I somehow knew she was my angel. Her aura was sparkling, almost as if someone had poured glitter over her. We paused in our walk and watched as a huge whale rose in the ocean before us. She reached for my hands and said: "Isaiah 41:10."

I woke up in the next instant and quickly wrote down the Bible verse so I wouldn't forget it. When I Googled the reference, I was comforted to read:

Fear not, for I am with you; be not dismayed, for I am your God; I will strengthen you; I will help you; I will uphold you with my righteous right hand.

The surgery went well and I was healed—not only from my cancer, but also from the doubts that often creep into my mind when I wrestle with my faith.

## THE BIGGER PICTURE

Spirit guides tend to help us with the daily aspects of our lives—our work, our relationships, our health and financial issues—whereas angels work to help us see the bigger picture, intervening to enlighten us about spiritual matters and our soul's growth. They like to serve as the wind beneath our wings, keeping our spirits uplifted when life brings us down.

Just this week, I had a powerful dream experience in which I was both a participant and an observer. I was one of several people standing with dozens of angelic beings. In a type of movie theater that was shaped in a semi-circle, we gathered around a middle-aged man named Oliver and showed him scenes from his life. I knew in the dream, as I simultaneously observed and participated, that Oliver was severely depressed and was considering suicide. It was clear that he was still alive; this was not a life review. We were attempting to help him see how meaningful his life was. As the angels flipped through scenes of his life, they kept telling him how special he was and how much his kindness mattered. While the angels spoke, the rest of us gathered around the man, holding him in the light.

At first, Oliver couldn't even look at the screen. His energy was filled with shame. I watched as scenes flickered of his much-celebrated and favored older brother achieving success on the football field and later, in the corporate world, while Oliver hovered in the background. His shame was rooted in this feeling that he was never good enough—not for his parents, not for his partner, and not for his Creator. His shame and regrets filled the theater with a potent, palpable energy.

But then the images flickered again, and we watched as Oliver opened his florist shop. One angel said: "You always remember customer's names and speak to everyone with such joy. That matters more than you can know." We watched as he put together a beautiful bouquet of lilies and tucked in a note for a customer who'd lost her husband. "Do you know how much that spontaneous gesture meant to her?" one angel asked. The scene flickered again to an image of Oliver snapping a leash on a dog and walking away from a shelter. "You saved that dog's life," another angel said. Then a new image of Oliver handing an employee an envelope of money appeared on the screen and I heard: "When you gave money to that woman after her husband lost his job, it helped put food on their table."

Finally, Oliver spoke: "I forgot about that." As more images appeared on the screen, he kept repeating: "I forgot about that too" and "I didn't even know that would matter so much." The angel standing closest to him said: "You matter, Oliver." I watched as she touched his chest and saw an arc of golden energy move from her hand to his heart.

Echo Bodine, a wonderful psychic, teacher, and writer, describes a vision she had in her book *The Gift*. She was in the delivery room with a friend who was giving birth when she saw a tall, male figure standing and watching the mother in labor, flanked on each side by two guides. The figure turned to his guides and said: "Okay, I'm going in. Keep me on my path." Then his spirit dove into the mother's body. In the next moment, she delivered a baby boy. This story reminds us that our guides and angels are always here helping us stay on our path and follow our soul's blueprint.

## HELP FROM THE OTHER SIDE

Sometimes we experience dreams peopled by unknown beings who seem to pop in to offer a word of advice or guide us to a solution we've been seeking. Very often, these beings aren't guides or angels, but merely interested souls who see an opportunity to help a fellow human being. This happened to Herman Volrath Hilprecht, a professor of Assyriology at the turn of the 20th century. In addition to teaching, he also went on expeditions to explore ancient Mesopotamian and Babylonian ruins. He traveled to Constantinople, where he volunteered to work in the Imperial Museum. To thank him for sharing his expertise, the museum director gave him sketches of two fragments of agate that were etched with characters. No one had been able to decipher the meaning of these two fragments.

Hiprecht spent hours trying to figure out the source of these fragments. Were they remnants of broken rings? Or could they be pieces of ceremonial figures? He could date the fragments to between 1700 and 1140 BC, but that was all. The rest remained a mystery to him until one night, when a Babylonian priest visited him in a dream. He later wrote to describe this dream:

A tall, thin priest of the old pre-Christian Nippur, about forty years of age, and clad in a simple abba, led me to the treasure chamber of the temple, on its SE side. He went with me into a small, low-ceiled room without windows, in which there was a large wooden chest, while scraps of agate and lapis lazuli lay scattered on the floor. Here he addressed me as follows. "The two fragments belong together. They are not finger rings, and their history is as follows: King Kurigalzu once sent to the temple of Bel, among other articles of agate and lapis lazuli, an inscribed votive cylinder of agate. Then the priests received the command to make for the statue of the god Nibib a pair of earrings of agate. We were in great dismay since there was no agate as raw material at hand. In order to execute the command, there was nothing for us to do but cut the votive cylinder into three parts, thus making three earrings each of which contained a portion of the original transcription. The first of the two rings served as earrings for the statue of the god; the two fragments which have given you so much trouble are parts of them. If you will put the two of them together, you will have confirmation of my words. But the third ring you have not found, and you will not find it." (*beliefgate.com*, Robert Moss)

When Hiprecht awoke and put the two fragments together, it read: "To the god Nibub, child of the god Bel, His Lord Kurigalzu, has presented it." Since the agate pieces were different colors, no one had thought before that they belonged together. Did this Babylonian priest journey thousands of years into the future to help Hiprecht discover the meaning of these agate pieces? Or does he exist in another dimension of time where he's still guarding the relics of his gods?

I had a fascinating dream in which I was standing in a giant cathedral. It was so huge that it felt bigger than our whole world. Inside this large, ornate structure was a massive organ. A man was giving me a tour of the cathedral. When we walked upstairs to look at the organ, he said:

> This is the music of the Universe. We all contribute a note to the organ each night while we sleep. What you contribute affects not only you but the whole world. This is the music from which the Universe sings creating the energy at which we all vibrate.

He then showed me a room filled with filing drawers and said: "Usually, souls come here each night and pick a note from a drawer." The notes in each drawer looked like piano keys, except they were oval in shape. Each file drawer had a picture on it to indicate the contents—pictures of a family spending time together, pictures of people hard at work, images of people exercising, or relaxing in nature, or expressing themselves creatively. Some drawers had pictures of the ocean, a nature trail, or a mountain. Others had symbols of emotions like joy, sadness, or peace. I noticed that some of the drawers even had pictures symbolizing negative events and experiences.

Before I could ask the man why anyone would choose a negative note to add to the Universe's song, he said: "Every night we come here and select our note for the next day. We are all responsible for programming the Universe with our energy." Then he led me out of the room, shut the door firmly, and motioned to a sign hanging on the door that said: "Closed."

The man explained that we were now moving into a different energetic vibration in which we have to choose and create our own note to add to the Universe's song. He then led me to a massive room that resembled a cafeteria with thousands of rectangular tables filled with people drawing or writing on blank notes. There was a basket on each table filled with blank notes and markers, pens, and paints. The man told me to take a seat and choose a blank note. He then said: "Now, more than ever, it's imperative that we all work together to create positive notes for the Universe to sing."

The dream left me feeling that we're all being guided right now to take charge of more than our own inner lives, which are crowded with our personal hopes and fears. We're also being asked to become cognizant of the energy we contribute to the world as a whole. When we're happy and positive, we create vibrations that pour out onto the people we encounter throughout the day. But when we're feeling angry, scared, or alone, this creates negative vibrations that cause those around us to feel similarly depressed.

When we open to the magic awaiting us in our dreams, we encounter our guides and angels, but we also meet deceased people who share our interests and have wonderful wisdom to impart. In order to develop a stronger relationship with your spiritual team, ask them for signs. Meditate at least once or twice a week with the intent of connecting with them. Give them permission to appear in your dreams. And, most importantly, thank them for their assistance. The exercise below is designed to prime your unconscious mind for a soul journey to visit your spiritual team for guidance and connection.

**Exercise: Connecting with Your Spiritual Team**
As you're falling asleep, put yourself into a relaxed state. If it helps, play meditative music like Steven Halpern's "Gifts of the Angels" or Gregorian chant. As you relax your body, imagine a ball of peaceful energy floating through your body from your head to your toes. Feel it acting like a sponge, absorbing all tension, pain, and worry from your body. Feel it soaking up all excess energy from your bones, tissues, and muscles as it floats through your head, neck, and shoulders, your back and torso, your hips and legs and ankles and feet. See the ball of light getting cloudy and gray as it absorbs all your anxiety and worry.

Imagine two green vines popping up from the ground below you. Visualize them entering the soles of your feet.

Feel the vines growing through your ankles, legs, and hips. As they reach your root chakra, imagine the vines meeting and blossoming into a beautiful red flower. Breathe in the color red and feel its passionate energy flowing through you. Visualize the green vines pushing through this red flower until they meet at your root chakra in the area below your navel. See the vines intertwining and exploding into a beautiful orange flower. Breathe in the color orange and feel its creative, life-affirming energy filling up your body.

Breathe the vines into your solar plexus chakra right above your navel. See them connecting again and exploding into a bright, happy, yellow flower. Breathe in the color yellow and feel its joyful, cheery energy flooding throughout your body.

Visualize the vines pushing through your chest and see them entwining at your heart chakra and opening into a pink flower. See the petals of this flower opening as you visualize pink and green light illuminating your whole body.

Take another deep breath and see the vines pushing through your chest until they meet at your throat chakra at the base of your neck and emerge as a light-blue flower. Feel the peaceful energy of this light-blue flower as it awakens serenity throughout your body.

Inhale deeply and visualize the vines growing through your head and meeting once again at your third-eye chakra. See them connecting and forming a rich, dark-blue flower. Feel this opening blossoming in your forehead and breathe in this beautiful indigo light.

Visualize the vines pushing out of the top of your head and meeting once more at your crown chakra as they blossom into a vibrant purple flower. See the petals of this violet flower opening and filling your energy with its purple light.

Breathe deeply and imagine the vines reaching up and out of your energy field, going high, high above you, all the way into the sky, until they meet again and connect in the form of a beautiful, pure white flower. Visualize the energy of this flower showering you with light from above.

Take another deep breath, pulling up energy into your body from the earth where these vines are rooted. Exhale feeling the sense of connection to all that is. Breathe in and feel the energy from above and below coursing into your body.

You are now connected to the Earth and to the Universe. As above, so below. You are connected and plugged into source. Send out a message to connect with your guide. Simply say in your mind: "It is my intention to connect with my guide in the dream state." Sit with this message for a moment and just maintain a sense of awareness. Be open to what you see, feel, hear, and intuitively know. If/when you make a connection, ask your guides for a message or any information you may need to know. As you're falling asleep, repeat to yourself: "I will meet my guides and angels in my dreams." Then choose a sign that will confirm the connection you have made.

In the morning, record any dreams you've had. Look for the sign you chose to pop up throughout the day as well. If you chose a red cardinal, for example, look to see a red cardinal throughout the day as further confirmation of your dream contact. Continue this gentle guided meditation until your guides and angels appear in your dreams. Often it can take several attempts for your energy and vibrations to clear and rise high enough to reach this realm in the dream state, but with consistency and intent, it will happen.

# Chapter 44

# REMEMBERING
# YOUR DREAMS

*Sleep is not just vital to health but perhaps the greatest single source of creativity*

Alex Tew

If you want to start working with the magic awaiting in your dreams, you have to start by remembering them. Everyone dreams, even babies in the womb. Studies have shown that the human fetus spends half its time *in utero* in the REM state. Adults generally have seven dreams each night, with the average one lasting from five to twenty minutes, although dreams lasting almost an hour have been recorded in research labs. If you follow the techniques outlined in this chapter, you'll become part of the 50 percent of people who remember at least one dream most mornings on waking.

Why should you try to remember your dreams? Not only are they the repository of your subconscious, enabling you to get in touch with deeper, hidden aspects of yourself, they are also a gateway to the other side, to astral dimensions, and to reservoirs of creative insights. Scientists, writers, artists, and inventors have all reported receiving intriguing, mystical information in their dreams.

## DREAMS OF DISCOVERY

Studies have shown that people who are predominantly right-brained tend to have better dream recall because the right brain rules our creativity, visionary thinking, and intuition. The left brain, on the other hand, governs analytical thinking and reasoning skills. Nonetheless, many scientists, who would most likely describe themselves as left-brain thinkers, attribute some of their best discoveries to dream recall.

Pharmacologist and psychobiologist Otto Loewi had a series of dreams that helped him understand nerve impulses, earning him the Nobel Prize for physiology in 1938.

> The night before Easter Sunday (in 1920), I awoke, turned on the light and jotted down a few notes on a tiny slip of paper. Then I fell asleep again. It occurred to me at 6:00 in the morning that, during the night, I had written down something important, but I was unable to decipher the scrawl. The next night, at 3:00, the idea returned. It was the design of an experiment to determine whether or not the hypothesis of chemical transmission that I had uttered seventeen years ago was correct. I got up immediately, went to the

laboratory, and performed a single experiment on a frog heart according to the nocturnal design. (*ncbi.nlm.nih.gov*)

Dreams also led to a discovery that would plague many of us in high school chemistry class—the periodic table of elements. After spending ten years trying to create a chart that would connect all the chemical elements, Dimitry Mendeleev had a dream that gave him the answer. He later wrote in his diary: "I saw in a dream a table where all the elements fell into place as required. Awakening, I immediately wrote it all down on a piece of paper."

A dream led Danish physicist Niels Boher to understand the structure of atoms. One night, he dreamed that he saw the planets attached to pieces of string traveling around the sun. After he awoke, Boher said he suddenly understood electrons and how they spin around the nucleus of an atom.

Dreams have led to fascinating developments in the world of mathematics as well. Srinivasa Ramanujan had little formal training in mathematics, yet his work led to almost 4,000 proofs and mathematical equations. His contributions to elliptic functions and number theory were well ahead of his time. He said all his proofs and theories were shown to him by the Hindu goddess Namagiri in dreams. He described one of these dreams like this:

While asleep, I had an unusual experience. There was a red screen formed by flowing blood, as it were. I was observing it. Suddenly a hand began to write on the screen. I became all attention. The hand wrote a number of elliptic integrals. They stuck to my mind. As soon as I woke up, I committed them to writing. (*famousscientists.org*)

A persistent series of dreams helped biologist and geologist Louis Agassiz make a fascinating fossil discovery. One night, after spending weeks trying to figure out the structure of a fossil fish, he dreamed that he saw the fish with all the missing parts fitted together perfectly. But when he woke and tried to hold on to the images, he lost the dream. He tried all day to recount the images from his dream, but to no avail.

That night, he dreamed of the fish again, but once more, couldn't remember it upon waking. So on the third night, he put a piece of paper and a pencil by his bedside. He had the same dream again, but this time—in total darkness and still half-asleep—he picked up the pencil and wrote it all down. His wife later recounted:

> With the drawing as a guide, he succeeded in cutting away the surface of the stone under which portions of the fish proved to be hidden. When wholly exposed, the fossil fish corresponded with his dream and his drawing, and he succeeded in classifying it with ease.

Albert Einstein had a revolutionary dream that helped him work out the theory of relativity. One night, he dreamed that he was walking past a farm, where he saw a herd of cows gathered against an electric fence. He watched as the farmer turned on the fence. In the dream, he saw all the cows jump back from the fence at the same time. But then he saw this same scenario from the farmer's point of view. The farmer saw the cows jump back one at a time as the electricity surged through the fence, forming a fluid wave motion. Einstein realized upon waking that things can look different depending on where you are and how long it takes for light to reach your eyes.

Nineteenth-century German chemist Friedrich August Kekule had been trying to figure out a structure that would explain benzene's properties when he had a dream that led him to discover the structure of the benzene molecule. After falling asleep on a London bus, he dreamed of a snake biting its tail forming a circle. Suddenly Kekule had his answer. Benzene is a ring of six carbon atoms. And it may have been a dream of a spiral staircase that led to the discovery of the double-helix structure of DNA by James Watson and Francis Crick.

## DREAMS OF INVENTION

What we focus on during the day often shows up in our dreams at night. When we're feeling anxious and hyper-focused on an issue, the answer to the problem often comes to us in a dream. This is where the old adage "just sleep on it" originated. If you give your conscious mind a question to ponder, it will be so busy trying to answer the question that it gives your subconscious mind free reign to explore alternative answers and insights. Many meditators purposely meditate on an unanswerable question to distract their "monkey mind" and allow their unconscious freedom to explore the "answer."

Elias Howe had spent years trying to invent the sewing machine. One night, he dreamed that cannibals surrounded him with spears demanding that he invent a working sewing machine or die. Upon waking, he recalled that the spears, which moved up and down, had tiny holes in the shafts. He suddenly realized what was blocking his invention. The threading needle required an eye—a hole in the needle's shaft just like the hole in the spears from his dream—in order to thread the bobbin. The result was a sewing machine capable of creating a lock stitch.

Jack Nicklaus said that a dream helped him learn a new golf technique that took ten strokes off his game. In his dream, he was holding the club in such a way that he was able to hit every stroke perfectly. In the morning, he realized that his dream had showed him that he was gripping the club incorrectly in his waking life. "I tried it the way I did in my dream, and it worked. I feel kind of foolish admitting it, but it really happened in a dream."

As we can see from these stories, sometimes anxiety can be helpful. Ever heard of the imposter syndrome—that feeling that you're not really entitled to be where you are in life? Well, thankfully for us, Larry Page suffered from it. He had an unfounded fear that he'd been admitted to Stanford University by mistake. After ruminating on this for weeks, he had a dream in which he saw himself downloading the entire contents of the internet onto his old computers.

When he awoke, he examined this dream and realized that what he had seen was actually possible. This led him to create what we now know as Google.

## DREAMS OF CREATION

There are dozens of stories from artists, writers, and musicians who were inspired to create their works in a dream. Perhaps the Greek myth of the nine muses has a spark of truth in it. The muses were daughters of Zeus and companions of Apollo, the god of music and the arts. It's said that these nine ladies visit Earth and whisper creative ideas and inspiration into the ears of artists who are open to receiving guidance. Nineteenth-century artist Sir Edward Burne-Jones even dreamed of meeting the nine muses on Mount Helicon. John Steinbeck relied on his dreams for artistic inspiration, saying in *Sweet Thursday*: "It is a common experience that a problem difficult at night is resolved in the morning after the committee of sleep has worked on it."

Perhaps the most famous story of a dream leading to a classic work of literature occurred appropriately on a dark and stormy summer night in Switzerland, when Mary Shelley was vacationing with her poet husband, her sister, and their friend, Lord Byron. Kept inside by the storm, they entertained each other by reading horror stories. Then Lord Byron challenged the group to create a horror story that was more frightening than the ones they'd just read. As Mary Shelley fell asleep thinking about this challenge, an idea came to her in a dream. She later wrote:

When I placed my head upon my pillow, I did not sleep, nor could I be said to think I saw with eyes shut, but with acute mental vision, I saw the pale student of unhallowed arts kneeling beside the thing he had put together. I saw the hideous phantasm of a man, stretched out, and then, on the working of some powerful engine, show signs of life and stir with an uneasy, half vital motion. (*Frankenstein,* Intro to 1831 ed.)

She began writing *Frankenstein* the next morning.

Movies like *Inception* and *Waking Life* were also inspired by dreams. A fevered dream that director James Cameron had one evening while fighting the flu gave us the terrifying image of a cyborg assassin. In Cameron's dream, he saw a huge explosion and a robot that had been cut in half emerging from the blast. The injured robot was carrying kitchen knives and heading straight for him. In the morning, he jotted it all down in notes that eventually led him to create *The Terminator.* Paul Schrader, who co-wrote *Taxi Driver, American Gigalo,* and *Raging Bull,* also attributes many of his movie ideas to dreams. In *Dreams—Understand Biology, Psychology, and Culture* (Valli and Hoss, 2019), he claims: "I often have dreams of sustained narration over a period of hours. These dreams have chapters, dialogue, and plot development."

Another fevered dream helped Robert Louis Stevenson create *Dr. Jekyll and Mr. Hyde.* He wrote about the experience in "A Chapter on Dreams," where he says that there are two of him—the one who votes, pays his taxes, and dresses respectably, and another self he calls a "brownie" or a familiar who was the true author of his writings. Once, while Stevenson was sleeping through a fever, his wife woke him when he began thrashing around and crying out in his sleep. Upon waking, he yelled at his wife: "Why did you wake me? I was dreaming a fine bogey tale." When he recovered, Stevenson wrote the now famous tale of a man with two very different personalities.

Stevenson called dreams "the little theater of the mind" and believed that all his best writing was inspired by brownies (muses?) who dropped ideas into his dreams. "My brownies do one-half my work for me while I am fast asleep, and in all likelihood, do the rest for me as well, when I am wide awake and fondly suppose I do it myself."

W. B. Yeats claimed the play *Cathleen ni Houlihan* came to him in a dream. He also claimed he had dreamed the poem *The Cap and Bells* "exactly as I have written it." William Thackery said he dreamed the title to his famous novel *Vanity Fair,* and A. C. Benson wrote the poem *Phoenix* in a dream he had in 1984. "I dreamt the whole poem in a dream," he acknowledged, "and wrote it down in the middle of the night on a scrap of paper by my bedside."

We can also thank dreams for giving us sparkling vampires. Stephanie Meyers dreamed of a girl lying in a beautiful field next to a vampire who was glittering in the sun's light. In the dream, she knew the vampire wanted the girl's blood, but she also knew he loved her deeply. She told one interviewer:

It was two people in kind of a little circular
meadow with really bright sunlight, and one of
them was a beautiful, sparkly boy and one was
just a girl who was human and normal, and they
were having this conversation. The boy was a
vampire, and he was trying to explain to her how
much he cared about her and yet at the same time
how much he wanted to kill her. (*Oprah.com*)

Ah, young love. In the morning, she wrote the whole scene
down, which we can now read in chapter 13 of *Twilight*.

Stephen King dreamed the plot line of *Misery* while
flying from Maine to England. He said:

I fell asleep on the plane and dreamed about a
woman who held a writer prisoner and killed
him, fed the remains to her pig and bound
his novel in human skin. His skin, the writer's
skin. I said to myself, "I have to write this story."
Of course, the plot changed quite a bit in
the telling. But I wrote the first forty or fifty
pages right on the landing, between the
ground floor and the first floor of the hotel.
(*thepsychologist.bps.org.uk*)

He also claimed that he:

. . . use[d] dreams the way you'd use mirrors to
look at something you couldn't see head-on, the
way that you use a mirror to look at your hair in

the back. To me that's what dreams are supposed to do. I think that dreams are a way that people's minds illustrate the nature of their problems. Or maybe even illustrate the answers to their problems in symbolic language.

Much of the music we love was also inspired by dream recall. When Paul McCartney was staying at the home of his then-girlfriend while filming *Help!*, he awoke from a dream remembering only a melody. He quickly ran to the piano to play it. McCartney later said:

> For about a month, I went round to people in the music business and asked them whether they had ever heard it before. Eventually it became like handing something into the police. I thought if no one claimed it after a few weeks, I could have it. (*storyofsong.com*)

At first, he didn't have words to go along with his melody, so he simply sang: "Scrambled eggs. Have an omelet with some Muenster cheese. Put your dishes in the wash bin please so I can clean the scrambled eggs." Thankfully, we all know that he changed those lyrics to create the beautiful balad "Yesterday."

In a 2011 interview with NPR, famous Rolling Stones guitarist Keith Richards says he actually recorded parts of a famous song while sleeping. When he awoke, he discovered he'd somehow written the first verse for what would become "Satisfaction":

I go to bed as usual with my guitar, and I wake
up in the morning, and I see the tape is run
to the very end. And I think, "Well, I didn't
do anything. Maybe I hit a button while I was
asleep." So I put it back to the beginning and
pushed play and there, in some sort of ghostly
version, is the opening lines to "Satisfaction."
It was a whole verse of it. And after that, there's
forty minutes of me snoring. But there's the song
in its embryo, and I actually dreamt the damned
thing. (*npr.org*)

## STRESS AND DREAMS

If we know that dreams can lead to the magic of discoveries, inventions, literature, music, precognition, and connection with the other side, then why don't we remember
every dream we have? Well, scientists are still researching
this question, but it most likely comes down to one fac-
tor—stress. Our brains are designed to protect us. When
we're faced with a stressful situation, our brains put us into
fight, flight, or freeze mode. What does this have to do
with dreams? Stress, it turns out, doesn't affect just our
waking lives, but our dreaming world as well.

If we're consumed with stress—from work, from parents, kids, or partners, from money woes or health con-
cerns—our brains produce copious amounts of cortisol.
Since cortisol levels rise naturally as we sleep, if stress has
increased our cortisol level throughout the day, then this
affects our dream recall.

Dreams are stored in the hippocampus. Sleep researchers Lynn Nadel and Jessica Payne published a study in which they point out that high levels of cortisol disrupt communication between the hippocampus and the neocortex. "This interruption of hippocampal-neocortical communication," they claim, "will halt the consolidation of aspects of memory. High cortisol levels could affect the nature of dreams," causing us to have bizarre or fragmented dreams and spotty dream recall (*ncbi.nlm.nih.gov*).

Clinical evidence has shown that high levels of cortisol sustained over time from chronic stress, illness, or trauma can significantly impair memory function and dream recall. However, a 2011 study revealed that people with higher Theta brain-wave activity after waking up are far more likely to remember their dreams. Since the Theta brain-wave state is connected to feelings of rest, peace, and serenity, this suggests two important facts.

The first is that you have a better chance of recalling your dreams when you wake up well-rested and when you can embrace moments of peace throughout your day. This means that, when you wake up Monday morning to an alarm clock screaming at you, a baby crying, or a dog barking to be let out, you probably won't remember your dreams. But if you awake on a Saturday morning to the gentle sound of rain tapping at your window and the delicious knowledge that you don't have to be anywhere that day, this relaxed state of mind will allow more dreams to bubble to the surface of your mind.

The second is that the more you can engage this Theta brain-wave state—through guided meditation, hypnosis, or deep breathing—you will not only reduce stress in your life, but you'll also strengthen your dream recall. I've kept a faithful dream record for over twenty years that has backed up this research. When I'm stressed over an issue in my life or am repeatedly awoken by a dog or a child needing my attention, I don't always recall my dreams. But when I'm focused on my spiritual life through daily meditation, Reiki, working with my crystals, and practicing yoga, my dream recall shoots up, leaving me feeling more engaged and connected with all aspects of my life.

If it's important to wake up feeling rested and relatively stress-free, however, it's just as important to fall asleep this way as well. Dream researchers tell us that, if you fall asleep exhausted, you're much less likely to remember your dreams. In fact, if you fall asleep within fifteen minutes of your head hitting the pillow, this is a sign that you're sleep-deprived.

On the other hand, you don't have to become a Zen Buddhist or monastic monk to recall your dreams. In my humble opinion, it's impossible to live a full life without stress or worry. I've had some of my most vivid and important dreams during times of profound stress. My "astral school" dreams began when I was pregnant with my third child and managing a hectic home life. There were only four or five nights a week when I actually slept through the whole night. So please don't read this research and think: "Well crap. You mean I've got to meditate an hour a day, practice yoga for another hour, and learn to fall asleep rested and wake up stress-free too?" For many of us, that's just too tall an order. However, it is a goal.

The more you can incorporate meditation, exercise, and mindful breathing into your daily life, the more easily you'll start to engage your dream life. If you can't do it every day, don't worry about it. Try meditating for five minutes on Saturday morning. Then move to twice a week and then three times a week, until you feel comfortable meditating for five minutes each day. Then expand this practice to ten minutes. If you do nothing else, you'll still reap huge benefits in your waking and sleeping life.

When I started meditating, I had three children under the age of four. I was teaching during the day and doing readings at night. I had a husband with a brain injury and was taking care of two dogs, three cats, two hamsters, and three goldfish. Not only did I not have time to meditate, I didn't have a "sacred space" in my home to accommodate this quiet time. I read so many books telling me to establish a meditation room. A room? I didn't have a square foot in my home that wasn't taken over by a Barbie doll, a Lego, or a dog toy.

So I created my "sacred space" in my closet—on a filing cabinet under a hanging row of shirts. I placed all my saint figurines and crystals on it and put a pillow in front of it. And that's where I meditated. I closed the door to my bedroom when the kids were napping and placed the baby monitor next to me. Sometimes, I actually got thirty minutes of uninterrupted silence, although it was usually more like five minutes. But it didn't matter. What paid off was showing up every day in front of my filing cabinet. Now, although I have much more time to meditate and have created a sacred space in my home, I still keep that filing cabinet to remind me that "where there's a will, there's a way."

## PRIMING THE PUMP

The wonderful medium John Holland always talks about "priming the pump." He says that we have to prime the pump through our daily activities to show up for spirit. But we also have to prime the pump to be awake and aware in our dreaming world. And meditation is the best way to do this. Not only has it been proven to rewire our brains, leading to more peace and inner joy, but research has shown that what we do during the day is also reflected in our dreams. If you spend a few moments each day focused on *you*—your spirit, your silence, your essence—this is going to show up in your dreams and lead to huge, magical, miraculous gifts of insights and connections.

It doesn't matter how you meditate, either. Don't let that word terrify you. Check out *Meditation for Fidgety Sceptics* by Dan Harris or *How to Meditate* by Pema Chodron. There are also wonderful apps on the internet. You can try a guided meditation or practice active meditation in which you focus on a word or mantra. I also love to practice passive meditation, just sitting in silence and observing any thoughts, feelings, or sensations that float to the surface. The key isn't *how* you meditate. It's *that* you meditate. As I say repeatedly on my podcasts: When you invest in you, the Universe invests in you too. When you take the time to carve out at least five minutes for yourself, the Universe takes notice and will also carve out time to focus on you and your needs.

Here are some tips on how you can adjust your bedtime routines to increase your dream recall.

- *Create a consistent routine.* If you're a night owl like me, this may be hard for you. I tend to do my best work at night. That's when I feel the most creative and inspired. But then I read an article about "revenge sleeping," which is when we push our bedtime off to grab a few more precious moments just for ourselves. But our bodies are tied to a circadian rhythm and function best on a consistent sleep schedule. We all need seven to nine hours of sleep each night. Anything less leaves us tired, but anything more can leave us lethargic. So aim for a consistent bedtime routine that works for you and manage your work schedule so you can get seven to nine hours of sleep each night. Do your best to maintain your sleep schedule over the weekends too. If you have to wake up to an alarm, try setting it to a gentler sound.

- *Do something relaxing.* Try to do the same thing each night before bedtime—like light stretching or journaling. Many like to use this time to focus on prayer or meditation. Avoid falling asleep to TV or with your phone next to you. Not only does the blue light effect your melatonin production, which helps regulate sleep, but these electronics also distract you and keep you awake much longer than you need to be. Taking a warm bath an hour before bedtime can also help you sleep better, because your body expends energy heating up and cooling down. This lower temperature signals the brain that it's time to sleep, leading to a better night's rest and improved dream recall.

- *Use a dream mantra.* Repeating a phrase to yourself as you're falling asleep has been shown to improve dream recall significantly. Try repeating "I will remember my dreams" at least twenty times as you're falling asleep.

- *Drink water before bed.* Drinking water increases your chances of waking up during your REM cycle, which has been shown to enhance dream recall. Only do this when you can grab some extra sleep in the morning, however.

- *Do concentration exercises.* Learning to focus the mind is a key aspect of recalling dreams. If you can tame an overthinking mind, you free up so much space for dream recall. Think of your brain as a computer whose cache and cookies have never been deleted. Practicing meditation and concentration exercises is like clearing these files and rebooting the computer. Try counting backward from 100 to 1 by threes, going from 100 to 97 to 94 and so on, until you get to 1. Or close your eyes and visualize walking through your home recreating every room and piece of furniture in your mind. Think of a word like "orange" and see how many words you can make from it. As you focus on pulling out words like "range," "ran," "gone," "rage," and "gore," your brain will slow down and focus.

- *Use dream herbs.* Consider making a dream bag to tuck under your pillow to facilitate greater dream recall. You can place dried mugwort, rosemary, lavender, and chamomile in a muslin bag. Or you can use these herbs as essential oils by placing them in a diffuser by your bed. All have been shown to enhance our dreaming life.

- *Ask for a dream.* If you're pondering an important decision or seeking guidance on an issue, write it down as a question and tuck it under your pillow. This helps you focus your mind on a task, freeing up your subconscious to seek an answer in your dreams. It also signals your guides to connect with you in your dreams. I've tried this throughout the years, and it always works—but never on the first night. I've noticed that it takes about a week for the answer to appear in a dream. So be consistent with this practice, because it works.

- *Work with crystals.* Certain crystals can facilitate better dream recall because of their pyroelectric and piezoelectric properties. Crystals can receive, hold, direct, project, and reflect light, so it makes sense that they can help us with our dreams. Crystal healers have noted that lapis lazuli, amethyst, unakite,

moonstone, amazonite, howlite, and selenite all help
with our dreams. Amethyst and howlite have been
shown to work together to prevent negative dreams
like nightmares. You can simply keep them by your
bed or tuck them under your pillow. I like to keep
mine in a drawstring bag with my dream question
and tuck it under my pillow.

- *Pay attention to your diet.* Eating a light dinner and
avoiding stimulants like nicotine or depressants like
alcohol before bed can lead to a more restful night's
sleep. Monitor your diet and see if certain foods help
or hinder your dream life. Eating a banana before bed
has been proven to help dream recall because bananas
are high in potassium and magnesium, which helps
muscles relax and creates a deeper sleep. They also
help raise serotonin levels, which has been shown to
help keep the brain more alert during the REM sleep
cycle, which, in turn, induces stronger dream recall.

Here are some tips for managing your morning routine in
ways that can facilitate dream recall.

- *Don't move upon waking.* When you first wake up,
do your best not to move. This jerks your soul back
into consciousness, causing most dreams to slip away
from you. Instead, lie in bed very still, keep your eyes
closed, and go back through your dreams trying to
remember anything you can. Don't push it or force
this recall. Simply allow your mind to become a
receptor of information filtering to the surface.

- *Keep a dream journal.* If you take away only one thing from this book, I hope it's the practice of keeping a dream journal. Well, two things. If you keep a dream journal *and* practice some form of meditation, you will see significant dream recall and experience an enhanced connection with your spiritual side. Mark each dream with the day, month, and year. It's fascinating to look back with the benefit of hindsight and see what your dreams were trying to tell you. A dream journal can also show you patterns in your life, like when you're most likely to remember your dreams. Some report having memorable dreams around the Full Moon. You may discover that you remember dreams best when you've had a light dinner or read a book before bedtime. Note the type of dream you have as well—precognitive, retrocognitive, lucid, telepathic, or symbolic. Commit to writing in your dream journal every morning. Even if you don't remember anything, write that down. If you only recall an emotion or color, write that down. If you awoke with a song in your head, note that as well. You'll soon see that the more you record your dreams, the more vivid your dreams will become for you.

- *Talk about your dreams.* This one can be hard, because so few people actually want to hear about your dreams. But if you have a friend or two who are willing to just listen, discuss your dreams with them. This can give you insight you may not have considered, and dream researchers have shown that talking about your dreams improves dream recall. Consider starting a dream group where you share and help interpret dreams together. If you can't talk about your dreams because they feel too personal, then simply journal about them.

- *Practice daydreaming*. Remember when you were a kid in school and spent so much time looking out the window daydreaming? Chances are you remembered your dreams more easily then too. When we allow ourselves moments of daydreaming during a waking state, letting our minds drift and wander, it primes our imaginations, leading to more visual dreams. If you have a hard time letting your mind wander, simply take a few minutes out of your day to stare out the window. Notice the colors, the movement of the wind, take in the sounds, make a note of your emotions. The more reflective you are in your daily life, the more reflective your dreams will become.

- *Engage your creative side*. Since science has shown that right-brained people remember more dreams than left-brained people, it makes sense that any activity you do that engages your creativity will enhance your dream recall. Working on a creative project is also a form of active meditation, because it strengthens your concentration and enables you to focus on the moment.

Dream research has proven that, when we wake up during the REM stage of sleeping, we are much more likely to remember our dreams. To help you wake up during this sleep cycle, you can set your alarm for about two hours after you fall asleep. Or you can set your alarm to wake you up two hours earlier than you need to be up. Fall back asleep for those remaining two hours and, upon waking, you will have a much greater chance of dream recall. As pointed out in chapter 7, most of our vivid dreams occur in the last two hours of sleep.

The artist Salvador Dali, famous for his surrealist images, slept with a key dangling from his thumb and fore-finger over a plate on the floor. When he fell asleep and began dreaming, his hand relaxed and the key fell onto the plate, waking him. This helped him remember his dreams and use them for inspiration in his art. Inventor Thomas Edison napped in a chair each day with two metal cake pans at his feet and holding two balls. When he entered the REM stage of sleep, his hands dropped the balls, causing them to crash into the metal plates, which woke him up. He claimed he got his best ideas from these dream naps. Edison, who was also interested in the paranormal, left behind notes that reveal that, shortly before his death, he was working on inventing a telephone capable of calling our departed loved ones in heaven.

## IT'S ALL ABOUT MOTIVATION

These techniques can all help you achieve better dream recall. But the best dream-recall technique can be summed up in one word: *motivation*. If you have the desire, the interest, and the motivation to recall your dreams, you will improve your dream life dramatically. When you set an intention and set your subconscious to focus on a task—in this case, remembering your dreams—your subconscious goes to work for you. Be careful, however, not to push yourself too hard. The subconsious mind needs time, permission, and peace to work best for you.

I like to think of my subconscious mind as a little man in my brain who's hard at work filing away everything I've processed that day. If I pester him too much, he gets overwhelmed and tosses the files, leaving me feeling scattered and fatigued. But if I give him the time he needs to file everything in his usual, organized way, then everything I need to recall comes to me at the perfect time. Give yourself grace and patience as you traverse the inner workings of your soul through your dream world.

With the right combination of meditation and motivation, you will soon be soaring through the dream time. As you explore the magic of dreaming and embrace the soul traveler you are, numerous gifts of spiritual understanding and awakening will be revealed to you.

So many of us go through life feeling happy and optimistic most of the time, while inside we often battle a feeling of homesickness, as if we're missing a home we never lived in or have an unspoken feeling that something is missing. Once I started connecting with my dreams on a deeper level, this "something's missing" feeling left me. I realized that my soul does return to its true home most nights. As soul travelers, we all carry a spark of the Creator within us and we can follow this spark of light home each night for connection, rest, renewal, and opportunities to heal and awaken.

Last night I fell asleep worrying about how I would conclude this book. I awoke this morning with a verse running through my head: "Like vagabonds we roam to distant shores unknown." When I Googled the verse, I found no author. Perhaps I wrote it in a dream I can't recall. Or maybe it was dropped into my head by one of the muses. We are all vagabonds traversing this Earth school together. But at night, our souls can connect, heart to heart, with hands clasped together, to explore distant shores unknown.

I wish you all sweet dreams, healing connections, and beautiful soul travels.

# BIBLIOGRAPHY

Barrett, Deirdre. *The Committee of Sleep*. New York: Crown, 2001.

Belanger, Michelle. *Psychic Dreamwalking*. San Francisco: Weiser Books, 2006.

Black, Joshua, et al. "Examining Dreams in the Healing Process Through Dream Bereavement." *Dreaming*, vol. 29, no. 1, 2019, pp. 57–78.

Bowman, Carol. *Children's Past Lives*. New York: Bantam, 2012.

Brown, Chip. "The Stubborn Scientist Who Unraveled a Mystery of the Night." *Smithsonian Magazine*, October 2003.

Burstein, Andrew. *Lincoln Dreamt He Died*. New York: St. Martin's Press, 2013.

Byrd, Randolph. "Positive Therapeutic Effects of Intercessory Prayer in a Coroner's Care Unit Population." *Southern Medicine Journal*, June 23, 2003.

Dossey, Larry. *Healing Words: The Power of Prayer and the Practice of Medicine*. New York: Harper Collins, 1993.

Fortune, Dion. *Psychic Self-Defense: A Study in Occult Pathology and Criminality*. Newburyport, MA: Weiser Classics, 2020.

Fox, Oliver. *Astral Projection*. London: Rider Publishing Co.,1939.

Gilchrist, Alexander. *The Life of William Blake*. New York: Dover Publications, 2017.

Graff, Dale E. *River Dreams*. Boston: Houghton Mifflin, 2000.

Guiley, Rosemary. *Dreams and Astral Travel*. New York: Chelsea House Publishers, 2009.

———. *The Dreamer's Way*. New York: Berkley, 2004.

———. *Dreamwork for the Soul*. New York: Berkley, 1998.

Hill, Napolean. *Think and Grow Rich*. London: Chatwell Books. 2015.

Hufford, David. *The Terror That Comes in the Night: an Experience-Centered Study of Supernatural Assault Traditions*. Philadelphia: University of Pennsylvania Press, 2010.

Jacobsen, Annie. *Phenomena*. Boston: Back Bay Books, 2018.

Jung, Carl Gustav. *Memories, Dreams, and Reflections*. Translated by Clara Winston. New York: Vintage, 1965.

Kirkpatrick, Sidney. *Edgar Cayce*. New York: Riverhead Books, 2000.

Knight, Sam. "The Psychiatrist Who Believed People Could Tell the Future." *New Yorker Magazine*. February 25, 2019.

LaBerge, Stephen. *Lucid Dreaming*. New York: St. Martins, 1989.

Lachman, Gary. *Jung the Mystic*. New York: TarcherPerigee, 2012.

———. *Swedenborg*. New York: Penguin, 2012.

Monroe, Robert A. *Journeys Out of the Body*. New York: Harmony, 2014.

Moss, Robert. *The Dreamer's Book of the Dead*. Rochester, VT: Destiny Books, 2005.

Muldoon, Sylvan Joseph and Hereward Carrington. *Projection of the Astral Body*. York Beach, ME: Samuel Weiser, Inc., 1973.

Nover, Lex Lonehood. *Nightmareland*. New York: TarcherPerigee, 2019.

Oberhelman. Steven. "Galen, On the Diagnosis of Dreams." *Journal of Medicine and Allied Sciences*." Volume 38, Issue 1. January, 1983.

Payne, J. D. "Sleep, Dreams, and Memory Consolidation: The Role of the Stress Hormone Cortisol." *Learning & Memory*, vol. 11, no. 6, 2004, pp. 671–678.

Rogers, Louis William. *Dreams and Premonitions*. Independently published, 1916.

Siegal, Bernie. *Love, Medicine and Miracles: Lessons Learned about Self-Healing from a Surgeon's Experience with Exceptional Patients*. New York: Harper Collins. 1986.

Smith, Carlyle T. *Heads-Up Dreaming*. San Antonio: Turning Stone Press, 2014.

Stevenson, Ian. *Children Who Remember Previous Lives. A Question of Reincarnation.* Jefferson, NC: McFarland. 2000.

Stevenson, Ian. *Twenty Cases Suggestive of Reincarnation.* Charlottesville, VA: University of Virginia Press, 1980.

Sugrue, Thomas. *There Is a River.* New York: Penguin, 2015.

Swedenborg, Emanuel. *The Lives of Angels.* Translated by George Dole and Lisa Hyatt Cooper. Westchester, PA: Swedenborg Foundation. 2013.

———. *Heaven and Hell.* Translated by George Dole. Westchester, PA: New Century Edition. 2010.

———. *Afterlife.* Translated by Donald Rose. Westchester, PA: Swedenborg Foundation, 2006.

Tucker, Jim. *Return to Life.* New York: St. Martin's Press, 2013.

Vedfelt, Ole. *The Dimensions of Dreams.* New York: International Publishing, 1999.

Voss, Ursula, et al. "Lucid Dreaming: a State of Consciousness with Features of Both Waking and Non-Lucid Dreaming." *Sleep*, vol. 32, no. 9, 2009, pp. 1191–1200.

Wilson, Colin. *Mysteries: An Investigation into the Occult, the Paranormal and the Supernatural.* London: Watkins, 2020.

———. *The Occult: The Ultimate Book for Those Who Would Walk with the Gods,* London: Watkins, 2015.

# ABOUT THE AUTHOR

Samantha Fey cohosts two popular podcasts, *Psychic Teachers* and *Enlightened Empaths*. After earning her Master's degree, she taught history and English before embarking on the spiritual journey that led her to receive her Reiki Master's degree and help teach others to embrace and understand their soul's purpose. Throughout her life, she's had vivid dream experiences which led her to study what happens to our consciousness when we sleep. She writes and teaches classes internationally on crystals, dreamwork, and intuition. She lives in coastal North Carolina with her three daughters, two dogs, and a library of treasured books and crystals.

# HAMPTON ROADS
# PUBLISHING COMPANY

*. . . for the evolving human spirit*

Hampton Roads Publishing Company publishes books on a variety of subjects, including spirituality, health, and other related topics.

For a copy of our latest trade catalog, call (978) 465-0504 or visit our distributor's website at *www.redwheelweiser.com*. You can also sign up for our newsletter and special offers by going to *www.redwheelweiser.com/newsletter/*.